IN THE HANDS OF GOD

BOOKS BY WILLIAM BARCLAY

Published by The Westminster Press

In the Hands of God
The New Testament, A New Translation
The Lord Is My Shepherd
Great Themes of the New Testament
Men and Affairs
The Men, the Meaning, the Message of the New Testament Books
New Testament Words
Introduction to the First Three Gospels
Introduction to John and the Acts of the Apostles
Marching On: Daily Readings for Younger People
Marching Orders: Daily Readings for Younger People
The Old Law & The New Law
And Jesus Said: A Handbook on the Parables of Jesus
God's Young Church
The King and the Kingdom
The First Three Gospels
Fishers of Men
Turning to God:
  A Study of Conversion in the Book of Acts and Today
Many Witnesses, One Lord
The All-Sufficient Christ: Studies in Paul's Letter to the Colossians
The Promise of the Spirit
Train Up a Child: Educational Ideals in the Ancient World
Daily Study Bible

IN THE HANDS OF GOD

by
William Barclay

Selected by Rita F. Snowden

THE WESTMINSTER PRESS
Philadelphia

Published by The Westminster Press®
Philadelphia, Pennsylvania

PRINTED IN THE UNITED STATES OF AMERICA
9 8 7 6 5 4 3 2 1

LIBRARY OF CONGRESS CATALOGING IN PUBLICATION DATA

Barclay, William, lecturer in the University of Glasgow.
In the hands of God.

1. Meditations. I. Snowden, Rita Frances.
II. Title
BV4832.2.B29 1981 242 80-25261
ISBN 0-664-24362-2

CONTENTS

Contents

CELESTIAL ERRAND BOY

If you had entered the London Central Y.M.C.A. at my elbow on a certain November day, you would have seen facing you a notice saying that Basil Oliver had died, and that his funeral was to be on the date given, and that during the next week there was to be a memorial service. You would naturally have deduced that Basil Oliver was a very famous man and a very important person, since his death was to be marked with such tokens of affection and respect.

In one sense you would have been right, and in another you would have been wrong. Everyone who knows about London Central Y.M.C.A. certainly knew Basil Oliver, but I don't suppose anyone outside had ever heard of him. I am sure that his Master Jesus Christ knew him very well.

Basil Oliver was eighty-five years of age when he died, and, if you liked, you could have described him as the oldest office-boy in London. Many years ago he lost his wife, and he came to London from the north. More than thirty years ago he came to stay in London Central Y.M.C.A. and since then he had never stayed anywhere else. When he stopped work, he made himself so generally useful about the place that a job was found for him. He collected the letters, went for the stamps, ran general errands, and did all kinds of odd jobs.

It was Basil who went and bought the Sunday newspapers for the other members of staff every Sunday morning. It was Basil who presided behind the tea and the coffee in the lounge on a Sunday afternoon. You couldn't be about the place for a couple of days without seeing him, cheerful, smiling, padding about in the rubber-soled canvas shoes he always wore, without an overcoat summer or winter, always stepping quickly about, kindly, ready to help anyone, and breathing goodwill.

He wasn't ill for long. For a week or two he was clearly failing; then one Sunday afternoon when he did not come down to serve in the buffet as usual, they went up to his room to see what was keeping him, and they found him unconscious on the floor. He died the next morning.

It is only now that we are discovering half the things that Basil Oliver did. Now we know that he directed boys about London, that he met them off trains, that he was ready with practical help when practical help was needed, that he did good for years without letting his right hand know what his left hand was doing; that, being dead, he yet speaks; that his works follow him.

Basil was a supremely happy man—you had only to look at him to know that. He was a supremely useful man—you had only to see him on his many self-appointed chores to see that. He did not make a parade of his religion—but the rector of the famous parish church of St Giles was proud to officiate at the funeral of one who never missed a service in his church. He was a supremely kind man—although he was not a rich man, and died with hardly a couple of pounds in his possession.

You see, the trouble of writing about Basil Oliver is that all the things he did were little things, that is, as the world sees them—but little things which mean so much. He is a brilliant example of a man who found both joy for himself and love from others by simply doing the little things that came to his hand in the place where life had set him.

He might have been a lonely man, but he had thousands of friends. He might have been an unhappy man, but he radiated happiness in helping others in simple ordinary ways.

Basil Oliver would have been shocked at the comparison, but I cannot help thinking of the conversation of two working-men heard on a London bus when the Rev. Dick Sheppard died. "So poor Dick Sheppard's dead," the one said to the other, and the other replied: "None of your *poor* Dick Sheppard here. God will be right glad to have him."

Those of us to whom London Central has become a home from home throughout the years, will not forget the little old man whom everybody knew, and who was never happy unless he was doing something for some one, who in the evenings used to sit in the lounge, a friend to all. And I am sure that his Master said to him when he arrived in heaven—still, I am sure, looking for something to do—"Well done, good and faithful servant; you have been faithful over a little, I will set you over much; enter into the joy of your Master."

If there is a job for a kind of celestial errand boy in heaven, Basil Oliver has it now! And he would rather it was that way, for a crown and a throne would only embarrass him.

WHAT IS THE POINT?

Rusty, our bull-terrier, likes nothing better than to get into the country. Give him a moor or a hillside and he is in his glory. But of all things, he likes water best. Take him to the seaside, and he will meet the waves one by one, the bigger the better.

Even more, he likes a shallow river or a burn. There, he seems to have one ambition—to remove all the stones from the bottom of it, and to lay them some considerable distance away on dry land. He sticks his head into the water, and nuzzles about on the bottom of the burn—I never can understand how he manages to go so long without breathing—and then emerges with a stone which he carries up the bank and carefully places on the ground fifty or a hundred yards away. *And he is back for more.*

He will do this for hours. I have seen him staggering out of burns with stones almost as big as himself; and, if he does find a stone he can't move, he nearly goes frantic. This afternoon, out in the country, Rusty spent almost two hours shifting stones from the bed of a burn.

Now Rusty is an intelligent dog—but I have always wished that he could tell me what's the point of all this. He never does anything with the stones; he simply goes on taking them out and laying them on the ground. It seems the most pointless proceeding anyone can imagine, but it is Rusty's idea of bliss.

What's the point of it?—that is what I would like to ask; and, when you come to think about it, it is a question one might ask a great many people as well as of a Staffordshire bull-terrier.

What's the point of so much of our business and of our hurry and our worry and our effort and our anxiety? We strive so hard to get a little more money, to get a little further up the ladder—and what's the point of it all? What good is it really going to do us? We trouble about this and that and next the thing. Even if the things we fear happen, the heavens won't collapse, and, as a friend of mine often says, it will be all the same a hundred years from now.

We would do well to stand still sometimes and ask: "What's the point of what I'm doing?"

I do occasionally wonder about many of the arguments that go on in committees and presbyteries and all kinds of bodies. It seems hardly an exaggeration to say that we can get all hot and bothered about a comma. A trifle can be magnified into a matter of epoch-making principle. It is beyond doubt that we would save time and trouble and wear and tear, if before we started an argument we would say: "What's the point of it anyhow?"

I hope that I won't be misunderstood, if I say that there is a great deal of scholarship of which one is sorely tempted to ask: "What's the point of it?" There are many books which have undoubtedly taken years of research, and which, regarded as pure scholarship, are monuments of erudition, but what's the point of them?

Epictetus used to say: "Vain is the discourse of philosophy by which no human heart is healed." It is an interesting test—and, if it were applied, quite a number of erudite works would emerge as vanity.

But there is a bigger question than any of these—

"What's the point of life?" Surely life is to know Jesus Christ, and through him to be ready fearlessly to meet the call of God when that call comes. If we saw life that way, then all other things would take their proper place.

Once Elijah ran away when things were difficult, and let no one blame him. But out in the desert there came God's voice to him: "What doest thou here, Elijah?" (I Kings 19.9) It might be no bad thing if every now and again we stopped and said: "What am I doing here?" It might enable me to see a little better what things are important, and what things really and ultimately and essentially do not matter.

WIDER HORIZONS

Yesterday I was at a conference of ministers in a holiday home in Ayrshire. Before the conference began, I was checking up on the lectern from which I was to speak. Now it so happens that I had been in this holiday home before, and I think that I must have used this lectern before, but for the first time I noticed a little brass plate on it. I carried it over to the light to read the inscription, and this is what it said: "This Church furniture, including the brass-work, was made by the members of 159 MU, during their spare time, for unit Church of St Christopher. The Church travelled from Egypt to Italy during the North African campaign 1941–43, when it was set up in Ismailia, Tripoli, Gioja del Colle, Brindisi and Naples."

And when I had read that, two things happened to me. I touched that lectern with a new respect, and I had a vision of the wider horizon of the Church.

Here I was standing in a peaceful Ayrshire sea-coast town, in a quiet, lovely house, but my hands were on a lectern which had seen the sands of Egypt and North Africa, the blue waters of the Mediterranean, the cities of Italy, and had gone with men who had fought and prayed and died.

It is good for us to get a glimpse of the wider horizons. It may be that one of the great dangers of the Church is the wrong kind of congregationalism—the kind that cannot see beyond the walls of the building in which it worships. The Church is bigger than that.

We have to think of the world-wide nature of the Church. I suppose that it is the literal truth to say that the Church is the only institution in the world which has in it members of every nation and country under the sun.

Men dream of world government in the political sense of the term. The only place in which world government comes anywhere near to realisation is the Church. It is not the possession of a nation or a country or a colour; the Church is as wide as the world, and even the tiniest congregation in the smallest village or hamlet in the most remote place is part of something which has gone out to the ends of the earth.

Secondly, we must think of the history of the Church. It is the simple truth that the Church existed before most of the nations which exist today.

When we sit at the Communion Table it is well to remember that we are sharing in the only ceremony in the world which has been observed somewhere every single day for something like the last nineteen hundred and thirty years. There is no continuity in the world like that. Nowhere are we so much in touch with history as we are in the Church.

And we do well to remember that in the Church we are more than in touch with the whole wide world; we are more than in touch with almost twenty centuries of history; we are in touch with eternity. In it we are always compassed about with the great cloud of witnesses. In it we are surrounded not simply by the greatness of time, but also by the infinity of eternity.

It may be that our whole conception of the Church is far too small and far too local, and far too parochial. John Oxenham wrote of the world-wide Church:

In Christ there is no East or West,
In Him no South or North,
But one great Fellowship of love
Throughout the whole wide earth.

In Him shall true hearts everywhere
Their high communion find.
His service is the golden cord
Close-binding all mankind.

Join hands then, Brothers of the Faith,
Whate'er your race may be—
Who serves my Father as a son
Is surely kin to me.

Let us at least look at the wider horizons.

LEARNING GLADLY

We are being presented with an astonishing phenomenon in our house these days. Jane, who is just ten years old, is busy learning modern Greek! She actually attends classes on a Saturday morning to learn modern Greek, and next Saturday she will have a test on it. She even goes to the Eastern Orthodox Church in Glasgow sometimes and shares in the entertainments which that church so happily provides for its children.

Of course, there is a reason for this. It is that a Greek family has come to stay three or four doors along from us, and there are two girls in it with the lovely names of Androulla and Dasoulla, with whom Jane has become very friendly.

There is another reason. It is that I have been fortunate enough to have as a student and a very close friend Father Athenagoras, the minister of the Eastern Orthodox congregation in Glasgow. Thus modern Greek entered into Jane's life.

Now I have been studying and teaching Hellenistic Greek for far more than half my life. I began learning Greek forty years ago now. Greek has always been my business; but, if I had suggested that Jane should begin a course of Greek, the suggestion would have been met with wails of protest and the most impassioned opposition!

What has set Jane on to modern Greek?

First and foremost, she is *interested*. She is interested in Greek because it is the language of her friends; and, as it happens, she is interested in Greek because the excellent teacher who teaches her in her day school has somehow implanted in the minds of her ten-year-old girls an amazing knowledge of the *Odyssey* and the *Iliad*, so that Jane walks familiarly with Hector and Priam and Paris and Helen and Agamemnon and Achilles and Penelope and Ulysses and all Homer's immortals.

The secret of learning is interest. There can be no real learning without interest. That is why the average boy has no difficulty in telling you the names of the football teams in any league in Britain, but is hopelessly stumped by a demand for a list of the kings of Israel and Judah. That is why he can tell you the scores in Test Matches and Cup Finals for years back, when the dates of far more world-shaking events are quite forgotten.

How to awaken interest is the problem which the teacher, and the preacher, will have to solve for himself, for the answer will be different in each case; but the problem of teaching consists far more in awakening interest than in transmitting knowledge.

Secondly, Jane is *learning with friends*. Learning is always better when it is done along with someone else. It is always easier to learn in a group.

Quintilian, the great Latin expert on education, was quite certain that education in a school was infinitely better than any possible private education, because of the friendship it provided and the incentive it supplied.

Luther used to say that Jerome's translation of the Vulgate was not a good translation, because he did it *alone*, and thus lost the promise that where two or three are gathered together, Jesus Christ is in the midst of them.

Thirdly, Jane has *a good teacher*. She has my friend Father Athenagoras to teach her. A good teacher must have three qualities. He must have enthusiasm; no one can produce interest in any subject unless he is interested in it himself. He must have joy; nothing communicates itself to a class like a weary fed-up-ness; and nothing irradiates a class like sheer *joie de vivre* in a teacher. He must have patience and discipline combined.

Scholars in the end like neither a slack teacher nor a tyrannical teacher. The ideal is the patience which never loses its temper and the discipline which earns respect.

Our basic mistake in our approach to education may well be the idea that the young person does not want to learn. In point of fact there is nothing in this world more thrilling than learning.

Awaken interest, provide a group of friends, find a teacher who loves his subject and who loves his scholars, and the problems will solve themselves.

THE POWER OF THE PREACHER

I was sitting in my club yesterday when a man I do not know came up to me and asked me about a certain famous preacher and theologian. He told me that he had been a regular army officer, and that on Sunday mornings when he found himself posted anywhere near, he used to slip away to hear this preacher.

Once he took his little niece along with him—about ten years of age. When they came out of the church, his first question was: "Well, what did you think of that minister?" "*Terrific,*" came the surprising answer. "*I had two sweeties with me in my pocket, and I clean forgot to eat them!*"

That is just about the best compliment I have ever heard to a preacher.

Wherein does this power lie? Someone has said that every preacher must try to give his people three things.

(a) He must give them *something to feel.* No great preacher was ever afraid of emotion. He must give the impression that this thing matters intensely, both to him and to his hearers; that it is in literal fact a matter of life and death.

A sermon cannot really be a pleasant and informal chat; it cannot be an innocuous moral essay; still less can it be a formality which has to be gone through. And yet it does sometimes give that impression. Rhadakrishnan, the great Indian thinker, once said of preachers and theologians of the West known to him: "Your theologians seem to me like men talking in their sleep." On the other hand, we must not forget the witness of one: "I preached what I did feel—what I smartingly did feel."

The preacher must feel the wonder of the Christian message. Only then can he stab awake the dull and listless hearts of men and women for whom a church service has somehow become a bore rather than a thrill.

(b) He must give them *something to remember.* To associate preaching only with feeling might well result in a kind of nebulous golden haze, very moving at the time, but transient in its effect. Hence the necessity of something to remember.

This is really to say that the preacher must also be

teacher; he must inform the mind as well as appeal to the heart.

It should for the most part be possible to sum up a sermon in one sentence. If we were asked after listening to a sermon: "Now, what was that all about?" it should be possible to put the essential content in a sentence.

If we may take another analogy, a sermon is more like a bullet than a charge of small shot. It should be concentrated rather than diffused. It should be so orderly and so intelligible that it should lodge immovably in the memory. And it is usually true that the man who is unintelligible is not unintelligible because he is "deep", but because he does not himself understand what he is talking about.

(c) But even if the preacher provides something to feel and something to remember, he has not completed his task. He must finally *provide something to do*. It must be a challenge to action, in regard to oneself or in regard to other people. A friend of mine used to say that every sermon should end with the spoken or unspoken question: "What about it, chum?"

Here exactly is the trouble, not so much about preaching, as about listening to preaching. It is a psychological fact that the oftener an emotion is stirred without accompanying action, the less likely it is that action will ever happen. It becomes in the end very easy to make emotion a substitute for action.

What a different world it would be if all the fine impulses were acted upon, if every time we felt moved to do something fine, we did it! This is indeed a case when we must strike when the iron is hot. The impulse is born, it glows and flames, but unless it is acted upon it cools and fades, and every time it is not acted upon the heart grows a little harder and the will grows a little weaker and action is less likely. One of the supreme spiritual dangers is emotion without action.

Something to feel, something to remember, something to do—the preacher who supplies these things will indeed be gladly heard.

JUDGE WITH CARE

Last Sunday night I had to travel by the night train from a town in the north-east of England to London. When I got on to the train at very nearly midnight, one other person got into the same compartment. He did not look the kind of person one would choose as a travelling companion. He had stained flannel trousers tucked into thick stockings and encased in vast gumboots; he had on a polo-necked sweater with no collar or tie; and he had not shaved very recently.

I looked at him, and decided it might be wiser to stay awake than go to sleep, for he certainly did not look the most respectable of citizens. It was one of the coldest nights of the year, in fact it was one of the coldest nights for years.

When the train reached York, my travelling companion looked at me and asked: "Would you like a cup of tea, sir?" I said that I would very much. He dashed out and came back with two cups of tea, and would not take any money. He then asked: "Would you like something to eat, sir?" Again, I said that I would very much, thinking that he had collected some sandwiches from the railway tea-wagon. But no, it wasn't that. He reached up to the luggage rack for his hold-all. He opened it, and out of it he produced a round, flat steak-pie which must have measured a foot across. He broke it in half, and presented me with one piece, and in spite of my protests, would take none of it back.

This young man, whom I had thought to be a danger, was one of the kindest people I had met for a long time.

And I want to add another story to that—something that happened on the Saturday night immediately before my night journey to London. I was staying in a large hotel in another town in the north-east of England.

Late at night the lounge was invaded by scores of teenagers in search of tea or coffee. I had been working at one of the writing desks at the top end of the lounge. I turned round. I saw a group of about twelve of them grouped round a table. One took something from his pocket, and with great care began to extract little pellets from the packet and to hand them round. They cupped them in their hands and sniffed them, before carefully placing them in their mouths. They then chewed them with every appearance of enjoyment.

I said to myself: "Pep pills! Drugs! Just what you might expect from irresponsible teenagers!" Then quite by accident I caught a glimpse of the packet as the lad who held it turned it over in his hand. It was *SenSen Cachous*, those harmless scented little pellets with which people have scented their breath since I was a boy, and long before.

These two experiences, on two successive nights, taught me to recall three rules:

(a) *Don't jump to conclusions.* If you do, the chances are you will jump to the wrong ones. An immense amount of harm has been done in this world by people drawing the wrong conclusions in their haste, and then putting about stories and suggestions quite untrue.

(b) *Don't make rash judgments.* In fact, don't make any judgments at all, at least until you have all the evidence. Of course, it is rank injustice to judge when you don't know all the facts. That is why the Bible tells us not to judge at all. Judgment belongs to God, for only God has all the facts.

(c) If you must judge others, *make sure you think the best of them, and not the worst.* However much we resent the worst construction being put on our actions, most of us are guilty of doing it to others. It would often make life a lot happier, both for ourselves and for others, if we were as determined to think the best of others, as we seem to be to think the worst.

"*Judge not that ye be not judged*" (Matthew 7.1.) It is a good word.

INVICTUS

I have a friend whose spirit I value very much indeed. He is a Scot, but he is a professor at one of the most famous English universities. He is one of the finest scholars, in his own line, in the country. He suffers from a handicap, however; he is very lame, and must always walk with the aid of two stout sticks.

I never, in all my life, knew a happier man. I never knew one who lived a fuller life. I have never heard him complain; I have never heard him refer to his disability with other than a laugh; I have sometimes even heard him talk of the advantages of being lame!

Now a short time ago, my friend had a fall and broke one of his legs above the knee. For an ordinary person that would have been bad; you would have thought that for him it would have been a disaster. The first letter I got from him after his fall was written in bed, and was an invitation to share the amusement which lying in bed could cause.

Of course, the break completely immobilised him for a time. But then he procured a wheel chair, and he proceeded to go on living and working as if nothing had happened. He became an expert at the forward and reverse movements needed to manoeuvre the chair to a place at the table.

I have lately attended two conferences at his university, at both of which he was in the chair! He controlled proceedings with characteristic discipline and humour. (One thing I must add is that he has a wife whose help is beyond all telling.)

I would like to call him Invictus, the Unconquerable. If there is one thing which rouses the human heart to admiration, it is the sight of a man who just won't be beaten, the sight of a man living not so much a normal life, but a super-normal life, with a handicap which might well have conquered him.

I had an experience when I was a student. I went to preach in a certain church. I was met at the door by a man. He invited me in, as if he were the host. He warned me of this and that step as we came to it; he led me round this and that corner, and brought me to the vestry. He showed me where to hang my coat, and where to find the pulpit hymnary and Bible.

"Now," he said, "let's choose the hymns for the service tonight."

I suddenly realised that this was the organist; and in that moment I also suddenly realised that he was blind. I knew that the church had a blind organist, but it simply never occurred to me that this man who was so solicitous, who knew where everything was, could be the blind organist.

Here again was a man I would like to christen Invictus, the Unconquerable.

I suppose that it is forgotten nowadays, but one of the most famous novels of its day was Walpole's *Fortitude.* There is one unforgettable sentence in that book: "It isn't life that matters; it's the courage you bring to it."

Adler, the psychologist, tells of two patients of his, both of whom lost their right arms. At the end of a year, the one man was a resentful, embittered, defeated creature, for whom the bottom had fallen out of life. The other was radiantly cheerful. He used to say that he wondered why on earth nature had ever bothered supplying us with two arms when one would do perfectly well. The one patient was defeated; the other unconquerable.

A pin-prick of trouble can reduce one to disgruntled hostility to life; a very avalanche of trouble can leave another with courage and cheerfulness completely unimpaired. There are people whom anything can knock out, and people whom nothing can knock out.

You remember Paul's words: "Hard-pressed on every side, we are never hemmed in; bewildered, we are never at our wit's end; hunted, we are never abandoned to our fate; struck down, we are not left to die" (II Corinthians 4.8–9. NEB). As J. B. Phillips puts it: "We may be knocked down, but we are never knocked out."

We can do a bit of self-examination here. There is no doubt which we can be—in Christ.

A GOOD PRIDE

In my morning newspaper was one of the pleasantest things I had read for a long time. Scotland has a new Secretary of State, Michael Noble. Yesterday Michael Noble was making his first speech in Parliament in his new high office. In the gallery there sat his eighty-three-year-old mother, and when her son rose to face and to answer his critics, the old lady clapped her hands and shouted out: "Hurrah for Michael!" Whereat she was removed by the Serjeant at Arms, and sternly reprimanded for "making a disturbance while the business of Her Majesty's government was in progress", and warned never to do it again!

Well, no doubt it was all against the rules, but I'm bound to say that I think that Lady Noble was perfectly right, and I wish that a whole lot more people would make the same kind of disturbance!

Every parent is proud of a child who does well. I am quite sure that a parent takes more joy and pride in the achievement of a son than ever he does himself.

Once, someone came upon Robert Louis Stevenson turning over the leaves of a scrap book into which had been inserted the press notices about his books. "Well," said the friend, "is fame all that it's cracked up to be?" "Yes," said Stevenson, "when I see my mother's eyes."

The pride and joy in his mother's eyes were his greatest reward. It is a strange parent who has no pride in a child who has done well.

Further, I think that every parent should show his

pride and joy when his child does well. Parents run a danger. The more they love their children, and the higher their ambition for them, the more they are apt to be critical.

There are parents, many of them, who give the impression of being afraid of praise. However well the child has done, they give the impression that they think that he ought to have done better. They allow their love for the child and their ambition for him to compel them almost ruthlessly to push on the child.

In many cases, a child would take an examination in his stride and think very little of it. It is the fussiness and the nervousness of the parent which upsets the child. In many cases, it is not the child but the parent who fails the examination.

No parent should be afraid to use praise. John Newton used to say: "I knew that my father loved me, but he seemed unwilling that I should know it."

Poor Mary Lamb, Charles' sister, had life punctuated by periods of madness. She knew when the times were coming, and she and Charles used to go hand in hand to the asylum where for a time she had to be confined. When she was young, she used to say despairingly: "Why is it that I never seem to be able to do anything to please my mother?" And maybe a parent's severity was responsible for much.

Martin Luther's father was so stern, so severe, and so critical that Luther was almost afraid to give the name "Father" to God. And when the reformer became a man, he used to say: " 'Spare the rod and spoil the child?' Certainly! But beside the rod keep an apple to give him when he does well."

This too has its lessons for sons and daughters. Youth is of necessity irresponsible. It is hard for youth to see that it is good for a man to bear the yoke in his youth. But often a young person will try to do well, simply because he knows that it will make a parent glad.

And the tremendous thing is that this goes beyond death. I knew a lad who had finished his course for the ministry, and was to be licensed as a preacher. With tragic suddenness his father, who had been very proud of him, died just two days before the licensing service was due. Of course, it could have been postponed under the circumstances. But I will not forget what the lad said: "Of course the service goes on. Dad will have a front seat in the grandstand tonight." Perhaps not very theological, but there speaks the accent of reality and of faith. For around us and about us is the unseen cloud of witnesses still looking down in pride on those they loved.

MAC, KEEPER OF BOOKS

A short time ago one of my closest friends died. His name was James Mackintosh, and he was the librarian of Trinity College Library, Glasgow.

Mac was a man who had played many parts in life and in the Church. He was trained in the law; he fought as a soldier in the First World War; he came back to take an honours degree in English; he went to be a missionary professor of English in India; he returned to the little parish of Newtonmore; and finally, for the last seventeen years he was librarian at Trinity College.

Within the College I was, I think, his closest friend.

For the last two years we travelled every morning to College together. The mornings will seem different when the day is not begun with the talk we used to have, while we sat for a minute or two in my car before we both went into College, each to his own work.

Mac never wrote a book, although he loved the English language, although words obeyed his bidding, although he was the most erudite man I ever met. But although Mac never wrote a book himself, there is many an author, and above all myself, who could not have written books without him.

Many and many a time I and many others would go into Trinity's spacious library and cross the floor to his little room. And then the questions would begin. "Mac, have we got such and such a book? Where can I find it?" And amidst the tens of thousands of books, he would put his hand on it. "Mac, where can I find this quotation?" And at least eight times out of ten he could tell you. "Mac, where can I find something about this or that subject?" And in no time he would tell you where to go for information.

Behind many an author's book there stands Mac with his love of books, his knowledge of books and his encyclopaedic knowledge, gladly and willingly placed at the disposal of all who would use it.

I sometimes think of the people who stand behind the figures who are in the public eye. In almost every case there is someone in the background without whom the work that everyone sees could not be done. In athletics it may be a coach or a trainer; in music or in drama or in singing or even in preaching, it may be a teacher; in business and even in politics, it may be a faithful secretary; with a son or a daughter, it may be a parent; with many of us it is a friend; and with still more of us, a wife on whom we depend.

Mac was one of these priceless people who stood behind, and many a book—all of my own—owed much to him.

Mac was seventy-six when he died, but he died seventy-six years young. He looked twenty years younger than he was, slim and active. I think that he was young because he lived in a world with treasures waiting to be discovered, and new things waiting to be known. Often from the ends of the earth requests for information about this or that would come to him, and Mac would start an investigation into his books and folios and pamphlets, and he would surface with a new collection of interesting things far beyond the original point he had been asked to discover or to establish. For him there was always interest, for there was so much to be learned.

A man will never grow old so long as he keeps the wonder of the world. However long he lives, life will still be new to him. To stop learning is the surest way to become old. That is why some men are old and tired and weary long before they are forty, and other men are still fresh and vivid and vital and alive and young when they are long past the three score years and ten.

Mac loved the hills and the sea. When he was over seventy, he was still climbing mountains and reaching the top. And it was in the little village where once he had ministered, and among the hills he loved, that death took him with merciful suddenness, just as he would have wished it to be.

He lifted his eyes to the hills and he saw God. And no one who ever heard him pray could doubt the closeness of his walk with God.

We shall miss Mac—and no one will miss him more than I. He lived close to learning; he lived close to nature; and he lived close to God. And there is none who can doubt that the name of the man who was the keeper of books is written now for ever in the Lamb's Book of Life.

ALL OF US

I suppose W. B. Yeats was one of the most musical and most mystical of modern poets. Anything less "made to order" than his poetry would be hard to imagine. But he himself, in a scrap of autobiography, gives us a curious glimpse into his work.

He had been ill, and his illness had left him lethargic and unwilling to work. He had gone to stay with Lady Gregory, and afterwards said that he owed everything to her. "I asked her," he said, "to send me to my work every day at 11 a.m., and at some other hour to my letters, rating me with idleness, if need be, and I doubt if I should have done much with my life but for her firmness and her care."

It sounds an extremely odd thing that anyone should say to a poet at 11 a.m.: "Go to your desk and write poetry", and yet that is precisely what Yeats did, and there is no poet in whom the stream of true poetic inspiration is clearer.

Beverley Nichols, in his first youthful autobiography written at the age of twenty-one, tells of a meeting with Winston Churchill. Nichols had just written his very successful book, *Prelude*. "How long did it take to write?" asked Churchill. Nichols said that he did not know; that it was done in patches over five months.

"Didn't you work at it regularly?" Churchill enquired. The young man said that he had found regular work impossible—that he had to wait for the mood. "Nonsense," said the great man, "you should go to your room every day at 9 o'clock, and say, 'I am going to write for four hours'."

Nichols dared to ask what happened if you could not write, if you had a headache or indigestion, and so on. Churchill answered: "You've got to get over that. If you sit waiting for inspiration, you will sit waiting till you are an old man. Writing is like any other job, like marching an army, for instance. If you sit down and wait till the weather is fine, you won't get far with your troops. Kick yourself; irritate yourself; but *write*; it's the only way."

To put it succinctly, Churchill believed that you could produce something like a work of genius using office hours, and he himself proved it. One of the difficulties of the work of the ministry is that, in fact, a man has no necessary office hours. There is no one but himself to see that he does his work. But there are certain things that he might well keep before his mind and his conscience.

First, there is a question. Is a scholar or a preacher going to accept a life in which he has to exercise much less self-discipline than a clerk in an office, a salesman in a shop, a worker in a factory? These people have to be at the desk, at the counter, at the bench at a certain hour. Why shouldn't he? Does the work of scholarship or the work of the ministry give or imply the right to begin work when we like, and to stop when we like? Is the very nature of our calling not such that we ought to be *more*, not less disciplined than the people to whom we minister?

And there is another question. What is the preacher

really thinking about while he is waiting for the mood, for the idea? Certainly, if he has no method in his preaching, he may be searching for an idea even late on a Saturday night. But the essence of the ministry is that a man does *not* preach as the whim or the preference takes him. He preaches his way systematically through the Christian faith, and through the Bible. The preacher ought to make quite sure that his people are receiving a balanced and proportioned and complete account of the Christian faith.

Immediately, this question arises. Does this mean that I must preach on things in which I am not interested, on things which do not attract me, on things which at the moment I know nothing about? That is precisely what it means—that your congregation may get from you more than the things you like, your pet subjects.

And if one man's experience is worth anything at all, I find it is the things one thought uninteresting that become filled with interest when one works at them, the books of the Bible seldom opened which become very arsenals of sermons when one studies them, and the things one knows nothing about that are very likely the very things one needs to know about. It takes self-discipline to do this, but as Churchill said: "It's the only way."

THE UNSEEN CLOUD

Not long ago I had the very great honour and privilege of preaching at the re-opening of Bloomsbury Baptist Church. I had come south without any pulpit gown, not realising that I would need one for the occasion. In the vestry, the other people who were sharing in the service were all gowned. And then Dr Howard Williams made a suggestion. He went to the vestry cupboard and he took out a gown, and said: "You can wear Dr Townley Lord's gown; it's still here." So I put on Townley Lord's gown, and I put it on with pride that I should be privileged to wear it, for Townley Lord was one of the great preachers and one of the great men.

Before preaching, I made reference to the fact that I was proud to be wearing his gown, for over many a year, the name of Townley Lord and Bloomsbury had been synonymous.

After the service, there was a reception in the hall below the church, and it was crowded with people. Then out of the crowd a lady came up to me. It was Mrs Townley Lord. "I'm so happy," she said, "that you wore my husband's gown today, and I'm so happy that you told the people, for it made me feel that Townley had a part in the service." Now whether I had worn his gown or not, it is quite certain that Townley Lord was one of the unseen cloud of witnesses compassing us about. The older one gets, the more one becomes conscious of the unseen cloud.

I have always remembered the thrill I had in preaching in the University chapel in St Andrews, and in being told that the very pulpit in which I was to stand, had been the pulpit of John Knox. As every day in my own class-room I step on to the rostrum, I remember the men who went before me in that New Testament class-room—A. B. Bruce, James Denney, W. H. Macgregor, G. H. C. Macgregor—what a company! Now when this kind of thing happens it has two effects.

It makes one very humble. It gives one a feeling of complete astonishment that one should be walking in such company. There is nothing like the memory of the unseen cloud to keep one humble.

Do we ever stop long enough to recall the great souls who were within the Church we know—the saints, the martyrs, and the prophets who were part of it? Do we ever think of the succession in which the humblest Christian walks? And do we ever feel how unworthy we are of all that has gone before? To remember the unseen cloud is to be humbled to the dust.

But to remember the unseen cloud is to be more than humbled—*it is equally to be challenged.* We have entered into the labours of other men; we must so labour that other men may enter into ours. The generations are each like links in a chain.

Am I lessening or am I enhancing the tradition which has come down to me? Do I bring joy or sorrow to the unseen cloud as they look down? When I meet them on the other side of death, will I have to meet their eyes with pride or with shame? No man lives to himself, and no man dies to himself, and no man can honourably forget those who have given him what he has, and in whose footsteps he walks.

If I am humbled, and if I am challenged, then still another thing emerges. I can only be true to them, I can only walk in their company, if I *in my life have the same daily and hourly dependence on Jesus Christ that they had.* The generations rise and pass away in the unending panorama of the years, but Jesus Christ is the same yesterday, today, and for ever (Hebrews 12.8). His arm is not shortened, and his power is not less. His presence is still with us, as it was with them, mighty to help and mighty to save.

And so the memory of the unseen cloud of witnesses fills us with humility that we should walk in so goodly a company, challenges us to live more worthily, and points us to the Christ whose grace was sufficient for them, and is today sufficient for us.

THREE-FOLD CONVERSION

In his book *The Lord's Creed*, George Ingle reminds us "someone once said that there are three conversions in a man's life—first to Christ, then to the Church, and then back to the world."

This is a very wise and penetrating saying. The first step in conversion is for a man to be convinced of the wonder of Jesus Christ, and to know that Jesus Christ can do for him what he can never hope to do for himself.

The second step in conversion is the conviction that this experience brings both the privilege and the responsibility of becoming a member of the fellowship of people who have had the same experience, and who share the same belief.

The third step in conversion is the awareness that we are not converted only for our own sake, that we are not converted to gain entry only into a society of believers, but that there is laid on the Christian the obligation to take upon his shoulders and into his heart the sin and the suffering and the sorrow of the world.

From this we can see three ways in which an alleged conversion may be incomplete and imperfect.

(a) A conversion is incomplete if it does not leave Jesus Christ in the central place in one's life. The shortest possible description of a Christian—a description with which the New Testament would fully agree—is that a Christian is a person who can say: "For me Jesus Christ is Lord" (Romans 10.9; Philippians 2.11).

Herbert Butterfield's words about facing the future are good: "Hold to Christ, and for the rest be totally uncommitted." Any alleged conversion which does not leave one totally committed to Jesus Christ is incomplete and imperfect.

(b) A conversion is incomplete if it does not leave one integrated into the Church. By this we do not mean any particular part of the Church; what we do mean is that conversion must leave one linked in loving fellowship with his fellow-believers.

Conversion is not something between a man and Jesus Christ, with no other person involved. True, it may start in that way, but it cannot end in that way. Conversion is not individualistic. It is in fact the opposite. It joins man to his fellow-men, and certainly does not separate him from them.

There is a certain kind of *so-called* conversion which separates a man from his fellow-men. It may fill him with a self-righteousness which rejoices in its own superiority to those who have no like experience. It may move a man to a Pharisaic self-isolation. There have in fact been not a few so-called conversions as a result of which a man has left the Church to belong to some smaller and holier body. The plain truth is that such a one should very seriously examine himself, if he finds what he regards as his Christian experience separating him from his fellow-men, or his fellow-Christians.

(c) A conversion is incomplete if it does not leave one with an intense social consciousness, if it does not fill one with a sense of overwhelming responsibility for the world. It has been said, and said truly, that the Church exists for those outside itself.

The Church must never be in any sense a little huddle of pious people, shutting the doors against the world, lost in prayer and praise, connoisseurs of preaching and liturgy, busy mutually congratulating themselves on the excellence of their Christian experience.

As soon as one is converted, he should be looking for ways and avenues through which to turn his experience into loving, caring action for men. His experience should have quickened as great a love for others, as he has for Jesus Christ. It is within the world that he tries to turn his experience into effective action.

These are the marks of the three-fold conversion that is real conversion.

SERVICE

A week or two ago, work took me to a very famous University city in England, and there I was put up at a famous hotel. I arrived in time for dinner in the evening, and, of course, when I ordered dinner I gave the waiter my room number—and there are well over one hundred rooms in that hotel, and all were full.

Next morning I came down to breakfast, and the same waiter was on duty at the table at which I sat down. As I ordered breakfast, again I gave my room number. The waiter looked at me with a pained expression on his face. "Of course, I know your number, sir," he said. "You are one of our guests. You were in to dinner last night."

When I came out of the breakfast room, I was crossing the entrance hall, and the head porter came up to me. "Your mail, sir," he said, handing me a pile of letters. I had only seen him in the passing when I came into the hotel the night before, and yet he knew who I was out of the hundreds of people staying there.

Ten days or so later I told this story to a porter in another hotel as far north as that one was south, to which work had taken me, and he looked at me in surprise. "But, sir," he said, "that would happen in any decent hotel."

Now it seems there is nothing unusual in these happenings. But—and here is the point—in how many churches would it happen! In how many churches would a stranger be recognised by name on his second visit?

Many a person can attend for weeks, and not be spoken to, much less be addressed by name. Anyone who has found it out, will likely have forgotten it. One has a much better chance of being recognised in the crowd in a good hotel than he has in many churches. Why is that?

First, the hotel people are interested in their guests as people and as persons. One of the odd and frightening features of modern life is the obliteration of the individual.

Paul Tournier, the great Christian doctor, is very much afraid of this tendency in modern medicine. In a great hospital a person tends to become a card in an index, or a case whose name is not even known. "If," he says, "I say to myself, 'Ah! There's that gall-bladder type or that consumptive that I saw the other day,' I am interested more in their gall-bladders or their lungs than in themselves as persons." They are cases, statistics, numbers, not persons. People tend to become "combinations of physical and psychological phenomena", rather than persons.

Tournier tells of an experience of a Dr Plattner, a friend of his. A woman came to him seeking an abortion. Always she referred to the child she wished destroyed as "a little collection of cells". She had completely devalued and depersonalised the child. Then one day Dr Plattner had an idea. "What name would you give the child," he asked, "if it were to be born?" The atmosphere of the conversation changed. The woman was silent; one felt that the child, as soon as she gave him a name in her own mind, was ceasing to be "a little collection of cells", in order to become a person . . . "It was staggering," concluded Dr Plattner. "I felt as if I had been present at an act of creation."

The essential of a real Church is interest—interest

which does not just see people as members or even as worshippers, but as persons with names.

And there is another thing which makes a good hotel good. It is the desire to be of service. Again, the odd thing is that in our civilisation this desire to be of service is a vanishing commodity.

A Church should want people—not just to add one more to the roll, but in order to do something for each. The motto of the Church should be that of the Church's Master: "Service!"

Unhappily, the image of the Church many have is that of an institution which is always wanting something from people, rather than of one passionately anxious to give something to people.

Why is that?

NOT FAR FROM THE KINGDOM

A journalist friend of mine sometimes very kindly passes on to me stories and incidents which he comes across in his work. I want to pass on one of his stories.

In a certain Scottish city, there was a lady crippled and house-bound. Some years ago she was given notice to quit her tiny house. She had no relatives; she had kept herself very much to herself; and now in her crisis she had no one to whom she could turn; and she could not think where help was to come from or what was to happen to her.

Her next-door-neighbour was a rough and ready bachelor in his fifties. He stepped into the situation. "Don't worry," he said. "I'll see you're all right."

He gave up his own house, searched until he found a two-roomed attic property. He gave his old neighbour one room, and he uses the other himself. He shares his home with the friendless old lady. He does her shopping for her. In his own way, he is the soul of kindness, and, as the old lady put it, he is always "a perfect gentleman".

A lovely story, but you see the story is not finished yet. In fact, the point is still to come. *The man who has done this and who is doing this is a notorious and militant communist.*

Life has its shocks, and they are not all unpleasant ones. Again and again the most unlikely people have a habit of emerging as the most improbable saints. Jesus knew that. The one man who helped a man in trouble on the road was a despised Samaritan. The one leper who came back to give thanks was another Samaritan. The one person who on Calvary still believed in Jesus was a criminal hanging on a cross. It would hardly be wrong to say that the first convert to the power of the Cross was a Roman centurion who thought that he was presiding at the execution of a revolutionary. Life has its surprises.

And not only has life its surprises, but quite suddenly out of things like that there flashes a truth which is a warning. It is not what a man calls himself that matters; it is what he is. It is not what a man says he is that matters; it is what he does. The man in the story called himself a communist; in fact he proved himself to have Christian graces.

If we are to accept the teaching of Jesus at all, then the only test of the reality of a man's religion is his attitude to his fellow-men. The only possible proof that a man loves God is the demonstrated fact that he loves his fellow-men.

In the parable of judgment, the basis of judgment is how a man reacted to the claim and the call of human need. The sheep and the goats are separated, not on the basis of the amount of Bible-study they went in for, or the amount of time they spent in prayer or even in the amount of time they spent in worship. They are separated on no other grounds than on the grounds of their reaction to human need.

The plain truth emerges that if a man does not find God in his fellow-men, he does not find God at all.

There are three lines of poetry:

I sought my soul, my soul I could not see;
I sought my God, but God eluded me;
I sought my brother—and I found all three.

Wilberforce was the man who gained freedom for the slaves, and whose selfless efforts banished slavery from all the territories which were then within the British Empire. Wilberforce had to suffer, and suffer terribly in the process, but he was consumed with the passion to find life for the slaves. A pious lady once asked him: "Is your soul saved, Mr Wilberforce?" "Madam," he answered, "I have been so busy trying to save others that I have forgotten that I had a soul to save."

The man who concentrates on saving his own life and his own soul will lose them both; and the man who is so concerned with an out-going care for others that he completely forgets himself, finds his life and his soul (Matt. 16.24, 27).

Let the communist in our story call himself what he will, and let him say what he believes and what he does not believe. I would be well content to take any chance with him on that day of judgment when God assesses the value of life a man has lived.

BELONGING

There is something in this morning's newspaper which I think has very much the human touch.

One of the people who lately lost his office in the changes in the government was Mr Selwyn Lloyd, the former Chancellor of the Exchequer. Now Mr Lloyd has a little daughter, Joanna, ten years old, and Mr Lloyd has often said that one of his regrets was the way in which public life left him little time for her. He tells how he told her that he was no longer Chancellor of the Exchequer.

She asked: "Are you going to be Foreign Minister again?" He said that he wasn't that either, that from now on he was just an ordinary Member of Parliament. Her immediate response was: "What a relief!" However many people regret Mr Lloyd's departure from office, one person will be glad, for his daughter will have her father back again.

Now it is just here that we have an illustration and example of one of the great problems.

One of the insoluble problems of a man who becomes a public figure is that *he no longer belongs to himself, nor to his wife and family*. He begins to belong to the public; and there is a very real sense in which that has to be so. A great surgeon cannot refuse to carry out an emergency operation because he happens to have planned a family party. A great police officer cannot refuse a sudden investigation of a crime because he would like to spend a night at home. A great statesman cannot refuse a tour of the country when he would much rather be with his family. A parson cannot refuse a summons to comfort the sorrowing and soothe the troubled and the ill, on an evening when he has planned an outing with his wife and children. The demands of public life are merciless and inexorable on the man who has something which the public needs and demands.

Now, this makes things very difficult for those who are nearest and dearest to him. Sometimes the human relationship collapses under the strain, as, for instance, in the tragic break-up of the marriage of Dick Sheppard, whose wife, in the end, left him.

Sometimes this relationship can be solved, as it was by Dr W. E. Sangster, the beloved preacher. Soon after their marriage, Sangster said to his wife: "I can't be a good husband and a good minister. I'm going to be a good minister." He seldom took his wife and family out; he often forgot his wife's birthday unless he was reminded; he spent much of his time on preaching and lecturing tours at home and abroad.

As his son writes in his father's biography: "It all depends, of course, what you mean by a 'good husband'. If you mean a man who dries up as his wife washes the pots, or a handyman about the house, or even a man who takes his wife out for an occasional treat, then my father was the worst of all husbands.

"But if 'a good husband' is a man who loves his wife absolutely, expresses that love daily, asks her aid in all he does, and dedicates himself to a cause which he believes is greater than both of them, then my father was as good a husband as a minister."

But the thing about Sangster was that he never ceased to love his wife and *to tell her so*. Only once in thirty years did she go away without him, and her train was not half-an-hour gone when he was sitting in the station waiting-room writing a letter to her, headed "On the first day of my desertion". On Easter Day. 1955, he wrote to her: "We don't give Easter presents. Easter is such a wonderful present itself. . . . What makes Easter so wonderful is the promise that we can belong to one another for ever and ever."

When love is great enough, and when love is expressed, the problem can be solved. In fact it is quite certain that many and many a man who belongs to the public could never do the work he is compelled to do were it not for the home in the background which he is so often compelled to neglect.

All talent is a responsibility, and the greater the talent a man has the less he belongs to himself. Jesus himself said that a man who put even the dearest relationships of life before Him, is not worthy of Him (Matthew 10.37-8); but where love is great enough, and where love lets itself be known, even this problem can be solved.

NO ONE SEES

I have in front of me just now the script of a BBC television programme. On the first page it reads like this: Setting and Lighting: 7.30–8.00 p.m.; Camera Rehearsal: 8.00–9.00 p.m.; Line-up: 9.00–9.30 p.m.; Record: 9.30–9.45 p.m. And the time on the air which the whole programme will take will be 4 minutes 35 seconds! There will be *two hours* of preparation and rehearsal for a programme which will last less than five minutes. And, believe me, if the programme is going to be effective on television it will need every minute of it.

This is typical and symbolic of how good work is done. It very often happens that the main part of some quite spectacular performance is never even seen.

A man may run a hundred yards in less than ten seconds, or a mile in less than four minutes, and quite literally the performance may have taken years of preparation.

A pianist or violinist may give a performance which will last perhaps half an hour, and there will be hundreds of hours of preparation behind it.

A spectacular aircraft flight, or a spectacular motor-car speed-record may be over almost as soon as it is started, and yet behind it there will be years of research and preparation.

It almost always happens that by far the larger part of some great piece of work is out of sight altogether. There is nothing more important than this long and meticulous preparation.

It is so with *preaching*. Preaching may look easy; it may sound fluent; it may appear spontaneous and in one sense effortless—but there will be hours of preparation behind it—or there ought to be.

There are preachers who, as they would claim, depend on the guidance and the inspiration of the Holy Spirit, and who despise preparation and might even say that preparation is not only unnecessary but also wrong.

Once Sangster, that great preacher, heard one of these preachers who never prepared but left everything to the Holy Spirit. "I never knew," said Sangster grimly, "that the Holy Spirit could be so dull and uninteresting."

There are times when it is next door to blasphemy to attribute to the Holy Spirit preaching like that.

This is not to say for one moment that there is no room for the Holy Spirit, and no room for spontaneity and for the inspiration of the moment; but it is to say that the better a man is prepared, the more the Holy Spirit can use him. The better the material, the better the use that can be made of it.

It is so with *public prayer*. He who leads a congregation in prayer must always remember that it is his duty to offer to God not so much his own prayers as the prayers of his people. He must therefore sit down beforehand and visualise the people and think his way into their needs, and come back with them to the throne of the grace of God. The man who refuses to make careful preparation for public prayer has little sense of responsibility and little involvement in the needs of his people. The prayer of the pulpit will depend for its effectiveness and its helpfulness on the way in which in private a man bears the troubles of his people in his mind and on his heart.

It is so with *life*. The foreground of life depends on the background of life. An ability to meet the challenges of life with courage, the tasks of life with strength, the sorrows of life with serenity does not just happen. A man's way of meeting life depends on what he brings with him to life.

You may remember the famous reply of Alexander Whyte of Free St George's, Edinburgh. Someone once said to him after a service: "Dr Whyte, you preached today as if you had come straight from the presence." And Whyte answered gently: "Perhaps I did."

An atheist was defined, I think, by John Buchan, as a man who has no invisible means of support. It is the man who comes to the foreground of life with a mind and a heart and a spirit prepared by contact with God in the background of life, who is really the master of life.

It is always true that the most important part of any achievement is the part that no one sees.

IN THE BACKGROUND

Lately I sat at an evening function at Trinity College in Glasgow. It was the closing evening and prize-giving of the course for laymen and laywomen, which meets twice a week throughout the six months of the first two terms of our college year.

It was the kind of function at which all kinds of people are congratulated and thanked for the services they have rendered, and the work they have done throughout the session. The director of the course made his speech. He thanked the Principal and the College for help; he thanked the distinguished and famous theologian who is convenor of the parent committee for all his encouragement; he thanked the equally famous and distinguished theologian who had come to present the diplomas and to speak to the meeting. He thanked all the teachers who had given their services throughout the session. And then he came to the end. There was still one person to be thanked—a person whose services had had much to do with the smoothness and the happiness of the running of the course. That person was the College janitor. If, he said, there was a better janitor in any college he would like to find him. All the many services required had been rendered with a sunny goodwill which made them doubly valuable.

Do you think it an odd thing that the thanks of the director should culminate in thanks to the College janitor? I don't. It was entirely deserved. When I come into the College in the mornings, I expect to find the place warm and comfortable. I expect to find my room as clean as a new pin. I expect my mail to arrive on my desk. I expect to find the carafe of water on my rostrum filled with fresh water, and the blackboard washed and cleaned. I expect to find the College door unlocked, and I expect to go down to the Common Room at 11 a.m. to find tea all ready and waiting. I expect to find the class bells punctually rung. I expect all that—and I get it. And there are something like a dozen other people teaching in College besides me—and they all expect the same—and get it.

If the janitor did not do his work, the whole place would be disrupted. In many ways he is the most essential man in the place, for unless his work is done, none of the rest of us could get our work done—and yet you won't find his name in *Who's Who*!

The more I think of life, the more I am impressed with our complete dependence on other people who do their jobs without ever being heard of. If my car goes wrong, I shout for help. I could not do my work for a day without my hearing-aid. When it goes wrong there is someone there to mend it in a matter of hours. It takes so many people in the background to enable any of us to go on doing our work. And the trouble is that we so often take them completely for granted.

You have only to think of so simple a thing as how we get to work in the morning. How different it would be if there was no wife or mother to get us out of bed in time, to get a breakfast cooked and on the table, and to see us out of the door in time to catch our train or bus! We seldom think of the man who drives the bus or the train, or of the policeman who directs the traffic as directly serving *us*. In fact, we seldom remember that the bus or the train has a driver!

I am quite sure that, far oftener than we do, we should stop to think how we are all bound up together in the bundle of life; that we should stop every now and again to remember our utter dependence on other people; that sometimes we should stop to look at our own work and to see in it, whatever it is, not something by which we earn a wage, but something which is contributing to keeping the world going, and something in which we must, therefore, take a pride.

We ought sometimes not only to thank God for our work, and our health and strength and knowledge and skill to do it; but also for the number of ordinary background people. Without them, few of us would be able to get any work done at all.

THIS NOISY AGE

The age in which we live has been called by many names, but I think that it might be truest of all to call it "The Age of Noise". There never was an age which had such a dislike of silence, and which so avoided silence at all costs.

Early this morning I had breakfast in a large London restaurant which is open very early, and a group of lads there had a transistor going full blast at one of the tables.

Shortly afterwards, I found myself in the lounge of a

London Club, and a group there had a portable radio providing music.

This evening, I was at a conference near London. And the chairman and I entered a minute or two before I was due to lecture. We sat down to wait for the right time, for we did not wish to begin too early and have late-comers interrupting. Before we came in, the room was a babel of talk; when we sat down at the table, the talk died to silence. Then—with still a minute or two to go—the chairman turned to the gathering and said: "Please go on talking. Your silence embarrasses me!"

That, of course, was only a jest, but it is strangely symbolic of the age in which we live.

I remember, when I was a boy, living in Motherwell. The house, attached to the Bank of which my father was manager, was right on the main street. My bedroom was in the front of the house looking down on to the street. Naturally, there was silence neither night nor day. At that time we used to go for holidays to Fort William, to which my parents belonged. And I still remember not being able to sleep at night for the silence. I missed the rattle of the tramcars, the sound of the railway-engines, and the noise of the traffic.

Today, we seem to wish to live against a background of deliberate noise. There are many homes in which the radio is on from the moment people get up until the moment they go to bed—not that they listen all the time, but they like to have a continuous background of sound.

There are certain things about this attitude of mind. If there is always a background of man-made noise, there are some things we will never hear.

I heard lately of a doctor who had actually to ask that a television-set should be turned off in a sick-room, so that he might hear the heartbeat of his patient through his stethoscope.

If you were out in the country some night with your car radio on all the time, you would never hear the nightingale. Not would you hear a cry for help in the night.

You cannot think against this background of noise. No man can concentrate, if he is trying to do two things at once; and no one can listen, even with the fringe of his mind, through this background of noise, and think and concentrate at the same time.

You cannot listen against noise. If people are always talking, there is no time to listen. One of the most important times in prayer, for instance, should be when talking ceases and one begins in silence to listen to God.

Perhaps we are coming to the reason for all this. This background of noise is perhaps a defence and an escape. Quite subconsciously, perhaps, we try to find a way to avoid thinking, listening, facing ourselves.

The truth is that it is often in silence the greatest things come. In perfect friendship we find it so. I sometimes go to a conference where one whole day is passed in complete silence, and it is very valuable.

Amidst all the thunder and crash, the most impressive sentence in the Book of Revelation is that which says that when the seventh seal was opened, "there was silence in heaven for about half an hour" (Rev. 8.1).

We need to remember in this age the words (Psalm 46.10) "*Be still, and know that I am God!*"

THE STANDARD

During the month of December I was staying for a week in an Oxford College. My rooms were very comfortable indeed; but on the second day I noticed the cleaning had not been done nor the bed made. I wondered if we were supposed to do our own housework, which I would have been perfectly happy to do. On enquiry, I found that a mistake had been made. So I spoke to the cleaner who was in charge of the part of the College where I was staying. I wasn't in any sense making a complaint or anything like that.

She was very upset about the whole business, and very apologetic. I said to her: "You needn't worry about it. I don't mind a bit. It doesn't matter in the slightest."

"Sir," she said, "it may not matter to you, but it matters to me that my work has not been properly done." That, indeed, was an answer. And that answer presents us with a very real and a very important question—*Who is it that you work to satisfy?*

Are you satisfied to push things through anyway and, if possible, to get away with as little work as possible? Or is there someone for whose verdict you care, and whom you wish to satisfy?

It seems to me that there are three people whom we must seek to satisfy.

(a) We must seek to satisfy *ourselves*. In the old days, a traveller was moving about in Japan. At that time, one of the specialities was inlaid wood-work, especially inlaid table-tops. The traveller visited the shop of a

Japanese craftsman. He saw there a table-top that he wished to buy, but the craftsman refused to sell. The traveller increased the money he offered. But the craftsman said: "It is not a question of money. There is a flaw in that table-top, and I won't sell it to you."

The traveller persisted: "I can see no flaw. No one could see any flaw. I'm willing to take it as it is, and pay you the price you ask for it." "No," said the craftsman, "I am not willing to sell it. Nothing imperfect is going out of my shop." And nothing would induce him to sell.

Every one of us ought to work to satisfy his own conscience. One of the tragedies of the present situation is simply the slow death of pride in craftsmanship. The first question we always have to ask of any job is: Does this satisfy me?

(b) We have to satisfy *an employer*. We talk much today of the responsibilities of employers to employees—and they are very real; but equally real are the duties of employees to employers. Kipling's prayer was that there might be men everywhere who do the work for which they draw the wage. The first point I would make with any student or any man is simply that he should earn his pay. The second question we must ask is: Am I doing an honest day's work?

(c) We have to satisfy *God*. God sees everything that we do, and, in the last analysis, everything is done for God.

There is a great story of David (in II Samuel 24. 18–25). David was instructed by the Prophet Gad to erect an altar and to offer sacrifice on the threshing-floor of Araunah. When he went to buy it, Araunah, for love of David, offered him the ground and animals for nothing. But the offer was refused: David was determined to pay the full price. "I will not offer burnt offerings to the Lord my God," said he, "which cost me nothing."

This is not simply a religious problem; nor is it simply pious and sermonic talk. In this modern competitive world, no firm can survive, and no nation can survive which offers shoddy and unconscientious workmanship—that which costs it nothing.

Here, as so often happens, religion and economics meet and agree. Both demand our best; *only then is it fit to be offered to God.*

A PERFECT GENTLEMAN

A number of years ago, a certain gentleman left a certain part of Glasgow to go to America. Throughout the years he has prospered in America, but he has never forgotten his own city. And at each Christmas time to this day he sends to Glasgow Y.M.C.A. a handsome cheque to give a Christmas party to the poor children of his own part of the city.

I want to tell you about two things that happened at that party, once this Christmas, and once a year ago.

Let us begin with the incident that happened a year ago. The children are many of them very poor; they turn up almost an hour in advance, waiting for the doors to open. It is worthwhile going a long way to see the joy on their faces when they sit down to their Christmas meal, and when they get their Christmas presents from the tree.

Last year a small boy, maybe seven years old, turned up. His name is wee Hughie. Wee Hughie had on a thin jersey and trousers and canvas shoes on the coldest night, and he was blue with cold. He had somehow or other fallen and scratched his face and the scratches had become infected, and they were covered with sticking-plaster, half on and half off. Wee Hughie was just a waif and stray who had found his way into the party.

He ate his meal; and then he got his Christmas present parcel. He opened it and on top was a bag of sweets.

I don't think wee Hughie sees sweets very often. Then he looked up and saw the secretary's wife and daughter sitting there, and wee Hughie crossed the floor with his bag of sweets held out: "Please," he said, "will you have one of ma sweets." Wee Hughie, the perfect gentleman, offered his sweets to someone else, before he would take one himself.

So this Christmas came, and there was the same party. The secretary was there again, and two of the little girls had attached themselves to him. They had come and said that they were shy and that they were afraid to go in among the other children. The secretary saw among the other children a figure he recognised. It was wee Hughie, a little bigger now, but although he had grown, his clothes hadn't grown with him, and even on a bitter cold night, there were two or three inches of bare skin showing between the top of Hughie's trousers and the bottom of his jersey.

The secretary called wee Hughie over and he came. The secretary spoke to him for a minute or two, and then, unasked and spontaneously, he took charge of the two little shy girls. He brought them into the circle, settled them in a good place round the Christmas tree and looked after them as if he was a host looking after his most honoured guests.

Wee Hughie, the tattered waif and the perfect gentleman, was at it again.

I don't suppose that wee Hughie is anywhere near being a saint or an angelic child; I am quite sure that he is as wild as the rest. Wee Hughie may sometimes be what is called a juvenile delinquent, but in him there is the natural stuff of which knights are made, and the courtesy which is the first attribute of a gentleman.

It makes you think.

It makes you realise that you daren't judge by externals. Look at the externals and wee Hughie is just a rather scruffy small boy; but beneath the externals there is a heart of gold, and as Burns said long ago, "the heart's aye the part aye that makes us right or wrong."

It is one of the queer paradoxical laws of life that you find the most amazing kindness among those who have least to give. It is an old, old saying that it's the poor who help the poor.

Long ago a Roman moralist said that the worst of wealth is that it is like sea water—the more you drink, the more you want to drink. The odd thing is that for many of us it is true that the more comfortable we become, the more selfish we become. So often, like the widow with the two mites, it is the people who have most who give least.

And in the end a question forces itself on the mind—what's going to happen to wee Hughie? He's going to grow up—into what? Are the circumstances of life going to make him a rebel against society, as so many from his background become? Is he going to grow up into one of those teenagers who are at war with society and with the police? Or, please God, is the knight and the gentleman going to emerge in the years to come? The Church, and the country, have a responsibility here.

IN ALL CONSCIENCE

In many ways it is true to say that a man is a creature who longs for authority. There is a real sense in which it is true to say that man longs to be told what to believe and what to do. But the trouble is that this longing for authority encounters so many conflicting voices even from the experts who are supposed to know.

A very simple thing made me think of this a few days ago. I was reading two newspapers, each of which has a column of medical advice to correspondents. In the one case, the medical adviser strongly insisted that two hours' sleep before midnight was worth four hours after midnight. He laid it down that everyone should be in bed long before the midnight hour.

In the other case, the medical adviser was characterising the saying that two hours' sleep before midnight was worth four hours after midnight, as an old wives' tale in which there was no truth whatsoever, and as a belief which should be decently buried.

What is one to do? When the experts differ so radically on so simple a thing, where is authority to be sought?

This is simply an example of the kind of problem with which we are so often faced. This leads us to think of the much wider problem of where, for the Christian, authority lies. There are many answers to that question.

(a) Does the authority for the Christian lie in conscience? There are those who have held that conscience is instinctive, inherent and innate. Epictetus used to say that no one is born with a knowledge of music or geometry, but everyone is born knowing the difference between right and wrong.

But there is no solution here. Conscience is a variable thing. The conscience of a child is not the conscience of a mature man. The conscience of a civilised man is not the conscience of a primitive man.

Even up-bringing makes a vast difference. One may be brought up in an atmosphere in which, for instance, total abstinence is a matter of conscience, and another may be brought up with an entirely different view.

And still further, it is perfectly possible that one may so silence, stifle and blunt his conscience that it ceases to operate as sensitively as it should. He can come to a stage when he can, without a qualm and without a pang, do what once would have troubled his conscience very much indeed.

Anything so variable and so much the product of circumstances as conscience, cannot be the final authority.

(b) Does the authority of the Christian lie in the Church? It does for the Roman Catholic. But the Church has been guilty of the cruelty of a Spanish Inquisition, of the unspiritual commercialism of a traffic in indulgences, of Pharisaic discipline, of rank obscurantism, and often of the total inability to make any precise pronouncement on the very things on which the ordinary man desires guidance, as, for instance, on the issues of peace and war. The Church on earth is far too human an institution to have any kind of infallibility attached to it.

(c) Does the authority of the Christian lie in the Bible? The trouble about the Bible is that no sooner have we quoted one text on one side, than it is often possible to quote another text on the other side. We could find authority in the Bible for destroying our enemies and for forgiving them, depending on which part of it we use. We could find authority for arguing that there is no life after death, and for arguing that life after death is the very centre of Christian belief, depending on whether we choose to quote the Old or the New Testament.

The fact is that there is no man alive who accepts every word of the Bible as authoritative. He is bound to select, and he uses some other principle to guide his selection.

The truth is that there is no such thing as a final authority which can be externally imposed on any man. It is God's method that man is compelled to his own mind, his own heart and his own judgment. And for the Christian there is only one authority and that authority is Jesus Christ, interpreted by the Holy Spirit. The Christian's questions will be—what does Jesus say about this? What does Jesus want me to do about this? How does this seem, read or looked at through the eyes of Jesus? What is the verdict of Jesus upon this?

Clearly this kind of authority comes from personal experience. You cannot tell what anyone will say about anything unless you know him; and we cannot tell what Jesus would say about anything, unless we know him and have his mind.

The final authority for the Christian is the knowledge of Jesus Christ, which is the product of the experience of Jesus Christ.

A TIME FOR JOY

Here in Trinity College in Glasgow, we have a pleasant custom. We invite well-known people to come and talk to us for ten or fifteen minutes after lunch. We get all sorts of people; and last week we had one who for us was an unusual kind of guest—Rikki Fulton, the comedian, at whom and with whom tens of thousands laugh all through December and right on to the end of March. And Rikki Fulton, like all great clowns, had something serious to say.

One thing struck me about him. I never met a man more thrilled with his job—more in love with it. "I don't want to make people laugh," he said. "I want to make them *shriek*!"

Even after a pantomime has been running for nearly four months, he said, he still couldn't wait to get on to the stage to make contact with his audience.

He told of the joy of receiving a letter from some saddened soul who, in the theatre, had found again God's good gift of laughter.

One could not help feeling the difference between this man eager in his job—sparing no pains to perfect it—and the dull, dispirited, dreary mood of some of us. There is a quiet serene vitality about this man that you would search for in vain in many a church.

And he had a message; his message was a moving appeal for the rediscovery of joy in the church.

How right he was.

I have been reading again a forgotten book—by

James Moffatt, *The Day Before Yesterday*. As usual, Moffatt is full of quotations from the widest range of sources. Again and again, he shows how religion has gained the reputation of being gloom-encompassed. Ibsen's Julian said: "Have you looked at these Christians closely? Hollow-eyed, pale-cheeked, flat-breasted all; they brood their lives away, unspurred by ambition; the sun shines for them, but they do not see it; the earth offers them its fullness, but they desire it not; all their desire is to renounce and suffer, that they may come to die."

You remember Swinburne,

Thou hast conquered, O pale Galilean,
The world has grown gray at thy breath.

There have not been wanting voices of protest.

Once Carlyle was propounding his favourite view that the worship of sorrow was the highest idea of moral goodness, and that it was to be found in the New Testament. Whereat Harriet Martineau turned on him with the retort: "I think Jesus Christ lived one of the most joyous lives."

Ruskin once declared: "We continually hear of the trials, sometimes of the victories of faith, but scarcely ever of its pleasures."

Sir Henry Arthur Jones used to say: "Morality is an uncommonly happy way of living."

There is in Christianity a two-fold danger; there is the danger of becoming too involved in the world, but there is also the equal danger of despising the world.

Baron von Hügel once said an extraordinarily true thing: "If there is one danger for religion, if there is any one plausible, all-but-irresistible trend, which throughout its long rich history has sapped its force and prepared the most destructive counter excesses, it is just that—that of allowing the fascinations of Greece to deaden or to ignore the beauties and duties of Nature."

Jesus loved the birds, and the lilies, and the crops, and the children playing games. There is a clear sense in which he loved the world.

The New Testament says: "Your joy no man takes from you" (John 16.22). It was Jesus' prayer that "his joy should be in his people, and that their joy should be full" (John 15.11). "Rejoice," says Paul, "and again I say to you, Rejoice" (Philippians 4.4).

The noun *chara* which means *joy*, occurs in the New Testament fifty-eight times, and the verb *chairein* which means to rejoice, occurs seventy-three times. The New Testament is the book of Joy. There is no excuse for the dull dreariness which so often passes for Christianity. We Christians are men and women who have received Good News from God. It ought not to take a comedian to remind us of God's ministry of laughter, and of the Christian duty of joy.

IN THE UNLIKELY PLACE

There are few books in the Bible which have taken such a beating as the Book of Esther. Again and again it has been pointed out that from beginning to end the name of God does not occur even once in the whole book. Again and again it has been pointed out that Esther glorifies Jewish nationalism and delights in the slaughter of the enemies of the Jews. Again and again it has been pointed out that Esther knows nothing of

Christian forgiveness, and delights in the most savage vengeance.

Even amongst the Jews, Esther's place in the Canon of Scripture was precarious. Some of the greatest Jewish scholars tried to give the book a kind of midway position. It was, they said, indeed produced by the Holy Spirit, but only for reading, and not as Holy Scripture. In point of fact, it was not until the Council of Jamnia in A.D. 90, that the place of Esther as a book of Scripture was finally assured.

In the Christian Church, Esther was viewed with still more suspicion. At the end of the second century Melito of Sardis did not regard it as Scripture, and, much more significant, when the great bulwark of orthodoxy, Athanasius, drew up his list of the books of Scripture in A.D. 367, he did not include Esther, and relegated it to the secondary books.

Luther, with his usual violence of speech, did not spare Esther. "As to the Second Book of Maccabees," he said, "and that of Esther, I dislike them so much that I wish they did not exist; for they are too Jewish and have many bad Pagan elements."

Even so sober a modern scholar as F. V. Filson says of Esther: "Something less than the highest standards appears in the Book of Esther. It reflects a good sense of the place of Israel in God's plan, but its militant nationalism and wholesale bloodshed are open to definite criticism."

Such then was, and is, the reputation of the Book of Esther. Now it so happens that a very short time ago I was engaged with a group of other people on certain work which involved this Book of Esther. Naturally we mentioned the things that had been said of Esther. And then one of the greatest living New Testament scholars who was there told us a story.

In the days of the 1914–18 war, a body of British troops were besieged for a long time. Boredom more than actual danger was the problem. Among them there was a man who was a man of culture, but an atheist. In the siege he missed above all something to read. In despair he went to the chaplain, thinking that he might have some books. All the chaplain had to offer was the Bible. At first the man declared that the Bible was useless to him; but out of sheer boredom he took it and began to read it. It opened at the Book of Esther. Now whatever else Esther is, it is a great story which would make a magnificent film scenario. The man could not lay it down until he had finished it. If the Bible was like this, it was a worth reading! So indeed he read on—and he was converted. And it is literally true to say that it was the reading of the Book of Esther which led directly to his conversion.

I think that I have told before of an army doctor who was converted by the reading of Leviticus, because its regulations for sanitation and for hygiene were so eminently sensible.

Now, if there are two books which, it is said, could be removed from the Bible without loss, these books are Esther and Leviticus—and yet in the two cases I have instanced these two books were the means towards conversion.

To put it simply—it is safer to leave the Bible alone! Almost the first person to criticise Scripture, and to pick and choose the parts he was going to dispense with, was Marcion who, as Tertullian said, criticised the Scriptures with a pen-knife. There is a tendency to do just that. No one is going to claim that the Book of Esther has the religious value of, say, the Gospel of John, or that Leviticus has as much of the gospel of grace as Luke. But the lesson of experience is that there is a place in Christian experience for all the books of the Bible, and even the books which seem most *unlikely* have been for some the way to God and grace.

We do well to leave the Bible alone in its entirety, for no one knows out of which book of it the Spirit of God will speak to the heart of some man.

HOW TO GROW OLD GRACEFULLY

When I was in London at New Year time, I was just about to cross a busy street when a hand was laid on my arm. It was a little old lady carrying a shopping bag. "Will you take me across the street?" she asked. "I'm too nervous nowadays to cross by myself." So I took her by the arm and helped her across the street. When we got to the other side she thanked me. I was just turning to leave her when she turned to look at me again. "*Never grow old*," she said, and vanished in the crowd on the busy pavement.

So this was her advice. She found old age so frightening, so humiliating and so generally unpleasant that her word to me was "Never grow old." There are many things to be said about that advice.

First and foremost, it is impossible advice. You may stop many things in this life and this world, but you cannot stop the years. You may keep it at bay for long enough, but you cannot stop the slow decay of bodily strength and the slow deterioration of the physical faculties. No man has yet discovered the elixir of perpetual youth. Carefulness will delay the process, but in the end it cannot stop it. The old lady's advice begins with the handicap of being impossible.

It is not only impossible advice; it is bad advice. Impossible advice is always bad advice, for it can only lead to frustration in those who try to take it. This is particularly so in the matter of which we are thinking. "There are so few," said Richard Steele, "who can grow old with a good grace." There are few more embarrassing sights than the sight of someone who is old trying to be young. There is nothing lovely in the sight of someone who is old, dressing, talking, acting, speaking in a deliberate attempt to appear young. You can say few more damaging things, for example, about a woman than draw attention to this weakness. There are few more valuable abilities in life than the ability to accept things as they are, and any wise person accepts the years without any resentment at all, for any wise person knows that it is possible to live in the attitude that the best possible age in life is exactly the age you happen to be.

And this means that the advice not to grow old is mistaken advice, for there is another side to the question and another aspect to the balance-sheet. Perhaps Robert Browning's best-known stanza is:

Grow old along with me!
The best is yet to be,
The last of life, for which the first was made:
Our times are in His hand
Who saith "A whole I planned,
Youth shows but half; trust God: see all nor be afraid!"

There are at least four things that the years should bring.

They should bring a sense of proportion. He must be a strangely unteachable character who fails to learn from the years what is important and what is unimportant.

They should bring an increasing serenity. Again he must be a strangely unteachable person who does not discover from the years that feverish haste and restless anxiety never did anyone any good.

They should bring also a larger tolerance. A man must be strangely blind if the years do not make him more sympathetic and more ready to forgive; for the older one gets, the more he sees clearly how he himself might so easily have made shipwreck of life; and when he sees someone else in trouble, he has surely learned to say: "There but for the grace of God, go I."

And lastly, surely the years will bring an increasing conviction of the triumphant adequacy of the grace of God. When we look back on life we see all that we have come through in the way of sorrow and of tears, of pain and of toil; and we know that we would not be on our own two feet today were it not for God's grace. The experience of the past must give confidence for the future.

The advice is not "Never grow old," but rather, "Grow old with wisdom and with God, sure that the best is yet to be."

IN THE PEW

One Sunday last summer, I worshipped to my pleasure and profit in Martyrs' Church, St Andrews. St Andrews is a world-famous holiday resort, as every golfer knows. During the summer months especially, many visitors find their way into the pews of the St Andrews' churches.

I was a stranger in Martyrs' that day. No sooner had I sat down than I noticed a little white card in the book-board in front of me, and I noticed that similar cards were laid out along all the book-boards. I took up one and read it, and my heart was strangely warmed. It said:

We welcome you to our Church and Fellowship and extend Christian greetings to you.

I did not feel a stranger any more.

After the service I told one of the office-bearers what a fine idea I thought it, and how much I personally had appreciated it, and he at once went on to tell me about two other cards used in Martyrs' Church.

The first is put into the pews on Communion Sunday, and it runs:

The minister, kirk session and congregation of Martyrs' Church, St Andrews, welcome you to the fellowship of the Lord's Table.

I know how touched I would have been to find that card in my pew had I found myself at Martyrs' on a Communion Sunday.

But perhaps the third card is the most original of all. It is a card which the members of this Church take with them when they go to other congregations, as for instance, when they are on holiday, and it runs:

As a visitor to this Church, I bring warm Christian greetings to all who worship here, from Martyrs' Church, St Andrews.

The card is thus received in the churches in which they worship.

I don't know who first thought of all this, nor how many other churches follow it—but isn't it a splendid idea? I wish that more congregations would take it up and practise it.

And now let me share three practical conclusions with which there may be some who will disagree.

The first card says that there can be no strangers at the worship in this Church. That is exactly as it should be. If that is so, there would be no such things as seat-rents in church; and no one should possess, as his or hers, eighteen inches of space. There should never be in any church even the faintest feeling that, if you go in as a stranger, you are sitting in someone else's seat.

It is perfectly true that, just as they do in their own house and home, people will get into the habit of sitting in a certain place; but there should never even be the suggestion that they have the right to do so to the exclusion of anyone else.

The second card says that there can be no strangers at the Lord's Table. I have always been unhappy about the system of "communion cards", as used in Presbyterian Churches, at least in Scotland, and I suppose elsewhere. I have always disliked the idea of a ticket of admission to meet a Lord who said: "Him that cometh unto me, I will in no wise cast out."

Still more do I heartily dislike the state of the stranger who happens to come to a church on a Communion Sunday, and who has to wait at the door while enquiry is made as to what congregation he comes from, and while a "visitor's card" is duly written out.

I know that a record must be kept; I know that elders must visit their districts; and I know that the Sacrament is for those who are pledged members of the Church. But in the last analysis, only God knows who are the members of his Church, and I do not know that the possession of a bit of paste-board guarantees that a man loves the Lord Jesus Christ and is in fellowship with his neighbour and his fellow-men. I do not like admission tickets to the Table of our Lord.

The third card says that we do not belong to one congregation, but to the Church. It means that, into whatever house we go, we still go into the same family. Now the practical conclusion that I draw is that, if this is so, if a man is unhappy and discontented in one congregation, the sooner he leaves it for another the better for the congregation and the better for him. In such a case let him find a congregation in which he will be happy, for he is not a member of a congregation, but of the Church, and all doors are open to him. The man or woman who worships with a grudge cannot worship at all.

There is a way to truly worship.

DEFINITIONS TO SUIT

Jill, the elder of our two grand-daughters, has a very bad cough and cold. One day last week she was in our house, and the time came for her to go home. My wife said to her: "Come on, Jill, put on your cardigan." But Jill didn't want her cardigan on, and wouldn't put it on. My wife said to her: "You've got a cold, Jill, and if you go out without your cardigan it will make it worse." Jill looked at her: "I haven't got a cold," she announced. My wife looked at her in astonishment because Jill's cold is obvious. Then Jill explained: "When you have a cold," she said, "your nose is wet. My nose isn't wet. What I've got is a cough. That's not a cold!" So, you see, Jill made her own definition of what a cold is, just to suit herself.

Now this is something that we all do. We all make our definitions to suit ourselves.

There is many a person who would be shocked at the idea of gambling who thinks nothing of "doing the pools" or "going to the bingo". This same person would be shocked to be told he or she was a gambler. All the likelihood is that this person would never go near a race-course and would never dream of entering a betting shop. People like this—and there are thousands of them—define gambling to suit themselves.

Gambling consists quite simply in putting your money to such a use that you may lose it, or you may get back a great deal more, without doing any work for it, and on the necessity that others should lose their money for you to get your winnings. Whatever way you do that, in a big way or a small way, it is gambling.

There is many a person who would be shocked at the idea of stealing, but who will readily fiddle an expenses account, or evade income tax. I have known people to adopt such petty subterfuges as to travel third-class and claim first-class expenses. The number of people who nowadays steal time that belongs to their employer is legion. Quite simply, stealing means taking what does not belong to you, and we cannot get away from that definition.

There are many people who would be horrified to be called liars; but they are quite capable of twisting the truth to suit themselves. They can invent a plausible story for being late for an appointment, or for forgetting to do something, or for failing to have something done when it ought to be done. They no doubt believe that they would never tell a deliberate lie; but they define what is a lie to suit themselves. A lie is simply a departure from the truth—and again that is a definition we cannot evade.

There are many people who would be shocked and appalled to be called murderers, and fairly certainly they would never strike a man down in cold blood or even in hot temper. But these very same people can gather round a coffee table, or meet for afternoon tea, or monopolise a telephone for minutes on end, quite deliberately murdering the reputation and the good name and the character of other people.

I often wonder if, when someone was repeating some spicy bit of gossip about someone else, we were to say: "Come on round at once and visit that person and let's ask if it's true," they would accept the challenge and come.

This kind of murder is the most cowardly of all, for the kind of person who does this, deals not in honest knock-down blows, but in treacherous stabs in the back.

I think that most of us at one time or another make our own definitions and make them to suit ourselves. It would be better for us and for everyone else if we were to face truth instead of evading it.

ON THEIR FEET

I wonder what our preachers will preach about on Sunday? Whatever else be in a service, I am quite certain that there is one thing which should never be out of it.

I know a house in Glasgow where three women met last week, one afternoon. One is herself ill, and can only keep going with the drugs her doctor prescribes. Not long ago, she lost her only daughter, at the age of twenty-one, electrocuted in bed by an electric blanket, a thing which, by all the laws of science, could not happen. The second had lost her nineteen-year-old daughter in a car accident. The third had lost her son, a brilliant young army officer and one of the finest lads I ever knew, in another car accident when he was coming home on leave from England.

Tennyson wrote in *In Memoriam*,

> *Never morning wore*
> *To evening, but some heart did break.*

Now what I want to ask is: Suppose these women—and thousands like them—go to church this Sunday, what are they going to hear?

They will not get much help from a denunciation of a current TV programme that offends, from a diatribe against Roman Catholicism, or an exposition favourable or unfavourable of *Honest to God*, or an exposition of what in the Bible you cannot believe and cannot accept. What I want to say is: *There should be no service of the Church in which the note of comfort is forgotten.*

Of course, people need rousing; of course, they need rebuking; of course, the Church must have its say on the civic and national and international problems of its day; but somewhere in every service there must be comfort.

Whoever else will be at the service, there will be someone with a broken heart.

It is extraordinary how mindful the Bible is of the broken-hearted. I turn to only one prophet, to Isaiah. "Comfort, comfort my people, says your God" (Isaiah 40.1). "I am he that comforts you" (Isaiah 51.12). "The Lord has comforted his people" (Isaiah 52.9).

You will remember how the prophet interprets his commission from God—and here none of the newer translations can ever really take the place of the Authorised Version. It is to bind up the broken-hearted: to give beauty for ashes, the oil of joy for mourning, the garment of praise for the spirit of heaviness (Isaiah 61.1–3). "As one whom his mother comforts, so will I comfort you" (Isaiah 66.13).

Sunt lacrimae rerum, said Virgil in that phrase at once unforgettable and untranslatable. There are tears of things. And the Bible never forgets the tears of things. And yet it can so often happen that a person can go to a service of the Church, and find that the note of comfort is forgotten.

If we are to preach on Sunday, let us remember that there will be those in sorrow there.

But even so, let us remember another thing. The Bible never forgets the older meaning of the word *comfort.* Frequently the Greek word is *parakalein,* and *parakalein* does not only mean to comfort; it also means *to encourage.* It is for instance used of soldiers encouraging each other as they go into battle.

It must never be forgotten that the Latin root of the word *comfort* is *fortis,* which means *brave;* and the true Christian comfort is no easy and sentimental thing, but something which puts courage into a man when life is threatening to take his courage away.

There is a sentence in Job which Moffatt translates with a flash of sheer inspiration. It is in the speech of Eliphaz the Temanite; and in it Eliphaz says to Job: "*Your words have kept men on their feet*" (Job 4.4).

How any preacher might covet such a verdict on his preaching!

In any service there should be that word of comfort which will keep men and women on their feet, still facing life erect and with steady eyes, even when life has dealt them a blow which threatens to leave them prostrate.

Let no preacher forget that, if he is to walk in the succession of the prophets, and if he is to bring the whole word to his people.

IN THE HANDS OF GOD

I have just come across some physiological facts. They are given as being true of the average woman, but I suppose that in general they will also be true of a man. The average woman owns 750 movable muscles, 500 of which work in pairs. Her skin covers an area of 20 square feet. "In any piece of her skin the size of a postage stamp there are four yards of nerves, a hundred sweat glands, fifteen oil glands, a yard of blood vessels, and three million assorted cells!" When you think of that, you can only say that in truth we are fearfully and wonderfully made (Psalm 139.14).

Now this is what we might call God working in a square inch; this tells us of the detailed marvel of creation; this is seeing God in the infinitesimally small things.

But then we go on to the other end of the scale, and we look at the universe. The astronomers measure the distance that stars are away in light years. A light year is the distance that light travels in a year. Light travels 186,000 miles per second. Therefore in one year light travels 186,000 multiplied by 60 for minutes, multiplied by 60 for hours, multiplied by 24 for days, multiplied by 365 for years.

Now the *nearest* star in the heavens is Alpha Centauri, which is four-and-one-third light years away. (That is to say, the nearest star to the earth is $186{,}000 \times 60 \times 60$ $24 \times 365 \times 4\frac{1}{3}$ miles away.) The Pole Star is four hundred light years away. (That is to say, its distance from the earth is $186{,}000 \times 60 \times 60 \times 24 \times 365 \times 400$ miles.)

Put this another way. The light we see shining from the Pole Star left that star just about when Shakespeare was writing his plays, when the Authorised Version of the Bible was being written, and has been travelling ever since at 186,000 miles per second to get here. And when we think of that, we can say with far more amazement than ever the Psalmist could, "When I look at the heavens, the work of thy fingers, the moon and the stars which thou hast established; what is man that thou art mindful of him, and the son of man that thou dost care for him?" (Psalm 8.3–4).

The point about all this is that we see God in two things. First, we see in God *the most detailed care.* Nothing is too small for God. God's love of detail can be seen in the delicate tracery of every snowflake. The very structure of the universe shows us a God for whose care nothing is too small. We need never fear that, as far as God is concerned, we are lost in the mass. The very form of the universe makes it easy to believe in a God whose love is over every creature whom his hands have made.

Secondly, we see a God of *infinite power.* Nothing is too great to be beyond the control of God. The immensities of the universe obey the laws of the universe just as much as the atom or the molecule do. Just as the issues of the individual life are in the hands of God, so are the issues of the universe.

When we come back from a mental journey through the universe, we can see its detail and be reassured that neither we nor those we love can ever drift beyond God's love and care; and we can believe that the issues of life and death can never be beyond his control.

We can be sure that each one of us, and all the world, is in the hands of God.

THE W.P.B.

There is a Church in which I sometimes preach, which has a very pleasant vestry. It is large and light and airy. It is well heated and comfortable even on the coldest day. It has a desk at which any man might be proud to work. It has a magnificent wardrobe to hold gowns and coats. It has an armchair and even a couch on which to relax. It has round its walls the pictures of its past ministers and kirk sessions to be an inspiration to the preacher in the present.

But amidst all its splendour there is one thing which this vestry does not have—*it has no waste-paper basket.* And that is a real loss.

A waste-paper basket is an essential part of life's equipment. There is an art, and a necessary art, of throwing things away. I suppose that the word *discard* must be connected with these card-games in which the presence of certain cards in your hand constitutes a handicap and a danger, and in which the aim is to get rid of them as quickly as possible.

In life there are certain things for which the waste-paper basket is the only right destination.

Paul speaks about putting away childish things (I Corinthians 13.11). There are some people who forget to grow up.

There is a colloquial phrase we sometimes use which has a good deal of sense in it. We sometimes say to people when we are appealing to them to be sensible: "Be your age!"

There can be habits and mannerisms which are attractive and endearing in a child or a young person, which can become merely irritating in an older person. There can be, for instance, a kind of pert vivacity which can be charming in a younger person but which becomes merely exasperating in an older person. There can be a consistent facetiousness which makes one laugh when one encounters it in youth, but which renders all reasonable conversation next door to impossible when it is found in an alleged adult.

It would be no bad thing to take stock every now and again, just to make sure that we are growing up, and that we are putting away childish things, that we are becoming mature and full-grown adults.

We must put away things which are out-of-date. Tennyson speaks of God fulfilling himself in many ways, "lest one good custom should corrupt the world."

Life is full of odd survivals. I write this on a Friday, and in Glasgow University we are looking forward to a holiday on Monday. We get a holiday on the third Monday of November, and on the third Monday—and Tuesday—of February. These two Mondays come precisely halfway through the Martinmas and the Candlemas University terms. We call them *Meal Mondays.* They are a survival of the days when students were very poor, and they were the days when the country and the highland students went home for another barrel of meal, and another barrel of salt herrings to see them through the second half of the term.

The necessity of any such journey is long since past, but we still get the Mondays as holidays—not that I would wish to alter that!

But the point that I am making is that this is a survival.

Now the Church is full of survivals. The language of the Church is archaic. The architecture of the Church is archaic, so that cathedrals like Coventry and Guildford are a sensation. Clerical dress is archaic; the Moderator of the General Assembly of the Church of Scotland still wears what is in fact eighteenth-century court dress.

For some extraordinary reason the Church moves in an atmosphere of antiquity. I have no doubt that it makes for dignity; I have also no doubt that there are times when it makes for complete irrelevance; for, if there is one thing that is true of religion it is that it must always be expressible in contemporary terms. Religion fails if it cannot speak to men as they are. It might be a salutary if painful exercise to see how much of the Church's methods could be consigned to the waste-paper basket.

We must also put away things which are sub-Christian. One would have a right to expect that Church meetings would be conducted with every bit as much efficiency as secular meetings, but in a quite different spirit of fellowship and unity. One would have a right to assume that in a congregation the problem of personal relationships would be solved in a way in which out in the world they are not solved.

There are few things which would do the Church more good than to give some attention to the waste-paper basket!

LET'S FIND REALITY

There is a tradition of the Gilbert and Sullivan operas, as the D'Oyly Carte Company maintains them.

Jane had her first experience of these operas on this present visit. When you are a Gilbert and Sullivan devotee, you wish to bring up the younger generation in the faith!

Jane saw two of the operas. She saw *The Gondoliers*, and she was charmed with it. And then she saw *The Yeomen of the Guard.*

The Yeomen is quite different from any other of the operas. It ends with the death on the stage of poor Jack Point, the jester who dies of a broken heart. The part of Jack Point was magnificently played by John Reed. But for Jane it was too realistically played, for the tragedy of Jack Point broke her young heart! She dissolved into floods of tears and wept bitterly the whole way home, and insisted that so long as she lived she would never consent to go to a Gilbert and Sullivan opera again.

That is not the only thing over which Jane weeps. Jane always weeps at the story of the Cross. In fact, she cannot bear to look on any dramatic presentation of the Passion. The story always makes her cry.

I wish there were more people like Jane. There are so many, so very many, who can listen to the Passion story, who can look at the Cross, and feel no answering sword of grief and pity pierce their hearts: who can look on these things with no more reaction than they would feel on hearing the fat-stock prices on the radio.

This has always been a problem. Tillotson, the great 18th century Archbishop of Canterbury, was one day talking to Betterton, the great actor. Tillotson asked Betterton: "Why is it that I, when I am preaching about the greatest things, leave people quite unmoved, while you, when you are acting in what is nothing more than a play, can move them to the depths of their hearts?" "Sir," said Betterton, "You are telling them stories, while I am showing them facts."

What a condemnation of human nature, what a commentary on the human heart, that the action of a play should be more real to people than the working out of the eternal drama of the love of God!

What is the reason for this? There are two, I think.

First, there is the deadening influence of familiarity. Most of us have heard the story so often that the cutting edge of it is gone. Secondly, there is the strange fact that for so many the Bible stories belong to a kind of land of make-believe. They happen in the same twilight land as the fairy-tales do; they lack the reality of events which are sharply historical.

How can this be amended?

It can be amended, I think, by new methods of presentation and communication. That is why people like J. B. Phillips with his new translation of Scripture, and Geoffrey Beaumont with his introduction of music in the modern idiom into the Church, are so valuable. That is why any man who finds a startling new technique of preaching, or of worshipping, is a man who is doing a public service.

Too often the Church is dying of dignity and perishing in the perfection of some noble liturgy. New things are apt to shock us, and we do not like being shocked. We much prefer to remain comfortably half-awake.

Instead of regarding those who discover new techniques of communication, and who adventurously use them, as dangerous semi-heretics, we should regard them as the new apostles of the age.

This is to say that we need re-expression of the Christian gospel; but even more than that, maybe, we need re-realisation of the Christian gospel. The re-expression is not an end in itself; it is only the means towards an end, and the end is the awakened realisation of what this gospel means.

Basically, the gospel message can never mean anything without one's reawakening to the fact of one's own sin, and the fact of the wonderful love of God, as expressed in the life and the death of Jesus Christ. It is when we face ourselves, and face Christ, that we are lost in wonder, love, and praise. We need to rediscover the almost lost discipline of self-examination; and then a reawakened sense of sin will beget a reawakened sense of wonder.

The ancient word rings out still: "*Is it nothing to ye all who pass by?*" (Lamentations 1.12).

HOE HANDLES

Apolo Kivebulaya was one of the great saints of the African Church, and in the book *African Saint* Anne Luck has told his story.

One of the most characteristic stories of him tells how he arrived at Mboga in the Congo. He was not the first missionary Christian to arrive there. Two African missionaries had been there before him, but they had had to leave because the people would not give them any food. These two former missionaries had been members of the proud Baganda tribe in which menial work is for women and slaves. So, when the people of Mboga refused them food, they had been far too proud to cultivate the land themselves, and so they had to starve or go.

Apolo knew this, and he was well prepared to grow his own food. As he passed through the patches of forest on his way to Mboga he stopped to cut some hoe handles to be ready to get to work on some patch of ground whenever he arrived. When Tabaro, the ruler of Mboga, saw Apolo coming into the village carrying his hoe handles at the ready, he said: "Here is a man who is going to conquer."

A hoe handle may be an odd sign for a conqueror and an odd crest for a victor, but the very sight of it marked out Apolo as the man who would conquer. And why? For the simple yet sufficient reason that here was a man who was clearly prepared to do a day's honest work. It is hardly an exaggeration to say that what the world needs more than anything else is men who are ready and prepared and willing to do an honest day's work.

But we can go a little further than that. Apolo's hoe handles made it clear to the Congo people that he was prepared to work as well as to preach.

Under the Jewish law the rabbis were the greatest scholars and teachers of their day; they were the equivalent of the modern professor. But every Jewish rabbi had to have a trade. No rabbi could take any money for teaching and preaching at all. He had to earn his living by working at some trade. So we find rabbis who were tailors, carpenters, perfumers, barbers; and we know the trade of one who might have become one of the greatest of all Jewish rabbis, if he had not become one of the greatest of Christians, for we know that Paul was a tent-maker, or, as the word probably came to mean, a leather-worker. The rabbi had to work with his hands as well as with his brain and with his words.

Tolstoi somewhere has a story of a nobleman who always kept open house. At evening anyone could come and have a meal at his open and hospitable table. And when anyone came, he was never turned away, but there was one test. The nobleman always said: "Show me your hands," and if the hands were rough and scarred with toil, then the man was given a seat of honour at the top of the table, but if the hands were soft and flabby, then his place was low at the foot of the table.

Dr Jacks somewhere has the story of an Irish navvy. He was a simple soul, and one day someone asked him what he would say if, when he died, he was stopped at the heavenly gates and asked if he could produce any reason why he should be allowed in. He paused for a moment, and then he looked down at his spade with its blade polished and sharpened with constant work until it looked almost like stainless steel. "I think," he said, "I'll just show them my spade." And doubtless it would be a passport to heaven.

Jacks went on to say that when he wrote his many books he always wore an old jacket; and the right sleeve of it had become all tattered and worn with the constant friction of his desk as he wrote. "I wonder," he said, "if my old frayed coat-sleeve will get me in."

One of the strange things about the ministry is that there are many people who do not really think that ministers do an honest day's work—and sometimes perhaps they could be right. There is nothing in this world more tiring and even exhausting than concentrated brain work and study, and there is nothing more emotionally draining than visiting people and trying to help them by nothing less than the giving of oneself. And in that sense there is no harder job in the world than the ministry. But the minister is self-employed; he has no one to see that he does his work efficiently and consciously, and in such a situation it is perilously easy to rise late and to fritter away time.

It always takes self-discipline to be a workman who has no need to be ashamed, and I am certain that there is no job where that self-discipline is more essential, and yet harder, than in the work of the ministry.

Let us remember that the man who is prepared to do an honest day's work is indeed the conqueror. There are some victories that we cannot all win; but the victory of honest work is a victory that is open to all to win.

ESCAPE OR VICTORY

I have just been reading the newspapers, and I find in them certain facts which command attention, though set down quite haphazardly.

In the last financial year, this country spent more on smoking and on drink than it did on housing, fuel and light all put together.

At the end of the dispute between Equity and ITV, the result in one case is that certain dancing-girls are to have their pay raised from £9 9s. to £29 8s. for a fully networked show. Almost at the same time, nurses in the great hospitals and infirmaries have been offered a pay rise of 2½ per cent, that is sixpence in the pound. It is therefore a very much more profitable line of business to dance than it is to care for the sick and the dying.

I find that a certain popular young singer estimates his income at £80,000 a year. Confronted with the fact that he gets eight times as much as the Prime Minister of this country, he says that he does not think that he is overpaid, but he does think that the Prime Minister is underpaid.

I find that an impressario tells us that when he is discussing terms with popular comedians, the talks must begin at a figure of £1500 a week; that figure serves as a basis for discussions. And I find a story of a comedian who cheerfully refused a contract for ten shows at £2000 a show, on the grounds that an extra £20,000 a year was no good to him, when the tax-man had done with it.

I then find a news item which tells me that the Milk Marketing Board has a proposal to tip a quarter of a million gallons of surplus milk down disused mine shafts this spring. When it is pointed out that this milk could possibly be powdered and then sent to Africa, where it could be used to cure 20,000 children from a disease which will cripple them, the answer is that it would be too expensive to install machinery to treat the milk in this way. One wonders what precise figure is "too much" to save the lives of 20,000 children.

When you read facts and figures like these, you might well be pardoned for thinking that one is living in a world which has gone completely mad.

The truth is that these facts paint a perfectly discernible pattern, and demonstrate a perfectly identifiable state of affairs.

It is quite clear that the world is prepared to give its highest rewards to those who entertain it. It will pay the entertainer far more than a doctor or a nurse or a statesman or a minister of religion or anyone engaged in the necessary work and services of life and living.

Entertainment commands the highest pay of all.

We may put it in another way. It seems that what most people are looking for just now is *escape*. What they want is anything which will enable them to escape from reality. The picture-house and the dance-hall provide an escape out of the hard world of reality into a world of romance and glamour. An entertainer provides an escape into laughter in which for a time the realities are forgotten.

W. M. Macgregor used to tell of a woman who lived in a dreadful slum in Edinburgh called The Pans. Every now and again she would go round her friends borrowing a little money here and there, and then she would go and make herself helplessly drunk. When others remonstrated with her about this, she would answer: "Dae ye grudge me ma one chance to get clain oot o' The Pans wi' a sup o' whisky?"

That the entertainer commands the biggest rewards of all, is simply proof that today men and women are engaged in running away from reality; the thing which they rate highest is escape.

Here the folly of this age stands out. Escape is a temporary thing; it may work for a moment or two or an hour or two or even a week or two; but in the end reality catches up on us, and reality has to be faced. And therein lies the greatness of Christianity;

for the Christian faith offers *not escape but victory.* It enables one not to run away from life, but to conquer life. "In the world you shall have tribulation," said Jesus, "but be of good cheer, I have overcome the world" (John 16.33).

The world offers escape; Christ offers victory.

THE STRANGER

Last night an American friend of mine was telling me about something which happened to him while he was in Scotland. My friend is an American minister; he is enjoying what you might call an extended vacation, and he is using it to take classes here in Glasgow University. He is a man of mature years, and has seen a good deal of the world.

He and his wife are staying just outside Glasgow, and they come in to classes each morning with a suburban train. Usually my friend is a bit early for his train, and he has got into the habit of talking to the porter in the station. He doesn't know even the porter's name, but he and the porter have a chat every morning.

One morning last week the porter came up to my friend and handed him a parcel, saying that he wanted him to have this. And what do you think was in the parcel? *A haggis!*

The porter is a Scot; my friend is an American. And the porter wanted to give the stranger within the gates a present from Scotland, and chose the most Scottish thing he could think of—and he just wouldn't take even a word of thanks.

It is a rather wonderful story. There's no wonder that my American friend thinks Scotland rather a wonderful place. But it is more than a story—it is a sermon!

If the Bible is certain about one thing, it is that we must be kind to strangers.

The Bible is very careful for the stranger. It is, in fact, interesting to bring together what the Bible says about the stranger.

No one must ever wrong a stranger. "You must love the stranger as yourself" (Leviticus 19.33–4; Exodus 22.23–9).

God loves the stranger, and so must we (Deuteronomy 10.18–19). "The Lord watches over the stranger," says the Psalmist (Psalm 146.9).

Again and again the stranger appears in the merciful laws of the Old Testament. The stranger must be fed and satisfied from the three year tithe (Deuteronomy 14.29). When the field is being reaped the borders must be left for the stranger, and the gleaner will not glean too closely but will leave something for the stranger (Leviticus 23.22).

There are few things God hates more than injustice to a stranger. "Cursed be he who perverts the justice due to the stranger" (Deuteronomy 27.19; 24.17). Prophet after prophet insists that one of the things which will bring about the doom of the nation is injustice to the stranger (Ezekiel 22.29; Zechariah 7.10; Malachi 3.5).

Hospitality is a sacred duty. "The stranger has not lodged in the street," says Job, "I have opened my doors to the wayfarer" (Job 31.30). In the parable it is the treatment of the stranger which is one of the things which settle a man's eternal destiny (Matthew 25.38, 44). The widows must be hospitable (I Timothy 5.10).

"Do not neglect to show hospitality to strangers," says the writer to the Hebrews (Hebrews 13.2). Hospitality and kindness to strangers are simple virtues, but the Bible sets them very high.

But another thing emerges from this story. Everyone who meets a stranger is an advertisement for his own country—and what an advertisement that porter was! You are bound to judge a country by the people of it whom you meet—and my American friend thinks all the more of Scotland because of the porter.

The opposite can happen. In the same group as my American minister friend, was an American girl. When she came to Scotland she rang up a certain famous institution in which a girl might have expected to find a welcome, and found instead such off-hand, cold and discourteous treatment that her whole idea of that particular institution has been lowered.

I wonder if offices and hotels and institutions at large realise how extraordinarily important the girl at the switch-board is? You can be received at the other end of the line with a cheerful :"Good morning! Can I help you?" or with a response which makes it quite clear that you rank as a nuisance! A stranger is bound to judge this way. There is more motion in the world than in any previous generation; there are, therefore, more strangers everywhere.

The Bible is in no doubt of our duty to them.

WE'LL THINK ABOUT IT

Jill, the elder of our two grand-daughters at three years of age, is a young lady with a mind of her own—and no small ability to express that mind. She knows what she wants, and she usually has a very good shot at getting it.

It so happens that Jill stays very near to us, and she spends a lot of time in our house, sometimes even electing to spend the night because she likes her Granny.

One night recently Jill was coming home in the car with her Daddy and Mummy and her small sister and her Granny. Jill said that she wanted to stay the night with her Granny. Her Daddy said: "Well, we'll think about it when we arrive at Cathcart." A little while later Jill made the same request and got the same answer. A little while later she made the same request, and again got the same answer. And this time she looked at her Daddy and said decisively: "*Don't bother thinking about it! Just let me!*"

And, you know, Jill had something, because this phrase, "I'll think about it", with its close companion, "We'll see", are curious phrases.

Often when we say, "I'll think about it," all that we really mean is that *we don't want to decide.* Very often the phrase is just an evasion, and an excuse for inaction.

There is a famous story of how in a moment of crisis in the history of Greece, Agesilaus, the Spartan king, assembled his men and prepared to go into action. He sent word to another of the Greek rulers asking him to come to help in the hour of their country's peril. The other king replied that he would consider it. Agesilaus sent back the answer: "Tell him that while he is considering it, we will march."

I think that we ought to be very careful that, when we say, "I'll think about it," we don't in fact mean precisely the opposite, and that we are not simply evading a decision that we ought to make.

Another way of putting this is that, when we say, "I'll think about it," we are often simply *postponing something that we ought to do.*

Committees can be very useful things, but it is not altogether untrue that a committee is a thing which keeps minutes and wastes hours! And sometimes one has great sympathy with the person who remarked that the ideal committee is a committee of two, one of whom is permanently ill!

Just sometimes we, perhaps quite unconsciously, labour under the delusion that if we talk about a thing for long enough, in some mysterious way we will find that it has happened. No one is going to deny the usefulness of thinking about things and of discussing them, but perhaps we should remember oftener than we do that thought and talk are in the last analysis no substitutes for action. There comes a time when talking and thinking must become doing, and when the phrase, "I'll think about it", ought to be left behind.

And, lastly, it is all too true that often, if we go on saying, "I'll think about it," the *thing will so often not be done at all.*

You might well divide all things into things which really do require thought before action, and things which demand action on the spot if they are to be done at all. Obviously, if a man fell into the sea and was in danger of drowning, the rescuer cannot stand and say,

"I'll think about it." He has to act on the spot or there will be no rescue at all.

It is often this way with some generous impulse. Someone's need moves us to pity and compassion; we would like to help; but we stop to think about it and the fine moment is gone. There is a Latin proverb, *Qui cito dat, bis dat.* "He who gives quickly, gives twice."

There is a time when it is no doubt wise to say, "I'll think about it," but maybe there are still more times when Jill is right, and when we ought to say, "Don't bother thinking about it! *Do it!*"

SERENE, HUMBLE, CERTAIN

John W. Doberstein in *The Minister's Prayer Book*, which I have been pondering, makes three quotations one after another, all on the same subject. Of the first two the author is nameless. "The life of the clergyman is the book of the layman," "The life of the clergyman is the gospel of the people." The third is from Kierkegaard: "Order the parsons to be silent on Sundays. What is there left? The essential things remain: their lives, the daily life which the parsons preach. Would you then get the impression by watching them that it was Christianity they were preaching?"

These three quotations are all saying something which has been said over and over again. They are saying that *the most effective sermon is a life*; they are saying that Christianity must be demonstrated in action rather than commended in words.

These three quotations all speak specifically of the

parson. But this is to limit the matter far too much. It is not only the life of the parson which is a good or a bad sermon for Christianity; the life of every Church member preaches or fails to preach for the faith which in words he possesses.

What then are the qualities which a Christian life should show? What are the qualities by which it ought to be distinguished and characterised?

In regard to *life* the Christian life should be characterised by *serenity*. The world is littered with people who, as one might say, are permanently disorganised. They are always fussing; they are always worrying; they are often in a near-panic; they never quite catch up with their work. All their days are rushed and harassed and hot and bothered.

There should be in the life of the Christian a certain calm. A worried Christian is a contradiction in terms. A Christian is by definition a man who has that inner strength which enables him to cope with anything that life can do to him or bring to him. There should be in the Christian a calm, quiet, unhurried and unworried strength which is the opposite of the feverish and fretful inefficiency of the world.

In regard to *people* the Christian life should be characterised by what the Bible in the Authorised Version calls *charity*. Maybe the best modern equivalent of charity is kindness. The Christian should be kind in his judgments; kind in his speech; and kind in his actions. It is characteristic of the world to think the worst, and to put the worst construction and interpretation on any action. It is characteristic of the world to say the cruel and the cutting thing; it is characteristic of the world to be so taken up with self that it has little time for kindness to others. But the judgments, the words, and the deeds of the Christian are kind.

In regard to *self* the Christian life should be characterised by *humility*. There are few things so common in this life as conceit, and there are few of us who are not fairly well pleased with ourselves. Humility really means the extinction of self. It is only when self is extinguished that a man can learn, for the first condition of learning is the admission of our own ignorance. Above all, it is only when self is extinguished that a man can really see the beauty and the necessity of service, and that he can discover that the essence of life is not in being served by others, but in serving others.

In regard to *death* the Christian life should be characterised by *certainty*. We are not thinking so much of death as it affects ourselves, although there is also the Christian who should be cleansed from all fear; we are rather thinking of death as it invades our circle and lays its hand on those we love. When death comes, so many people are submerged in sorrow; so many are left in a state of collapse; so many grow bitter and resentful; so many live as if all that they were left with is memory, and as if there were no hope. The Christian is the man who in life's bitterest hour is still certain that nothing in life or in death can separate him from those whom he loved, and from the love of God in Christ Jesus his Lord.

With regard to life, *serenity*, with regard to people, *charity*, with regard to self, *humility*, with regard to death, *certainty*—these are the characteristics of the Christian life.

THINGS THAT COUNT

I borrow this story from the *Sunday Post*, which borrowed it from the Kilmadock Kirk Magazine.

There was a kirk which was looking for a minister. The vacancy committee was at the stage when it was sifting its way through the applications. The committee listened attentively as the clerk read them one by one.

All the candidates, with one exception, seemed to be gentlemen of the highest moral character—brilliant orators, tireless pastors, and experts at reviving flagging congregations and making misers glad to give.

The application which was different from the others went like this: "I have preached in a number of small churches, mostly situated in big towns, but I have never been in one place for more than three years. I have had some success as an author. My relationships with certain church officials in towns where I have preached have not always been of the best, and some of these office-bearers actually threatened me. I have been in jail three or four times for causing a breach of the peace. I am over fifty years of age, and my health is not very good. My memory is rather poor. Indeed, I have been known to forget the names of those whom I have baptised. Nevertheless, I still get quite a lot done. If you can see your way to appointing me, I shall do my best for you."

"Good heavens," said the interim-moderator, "appoint an unhealthy, trouble-making, absent-minded jail-bird? Who on earth is the fellow?"

"Well, sir," replied the clerk, "he signs himself 'Paul'!"

That is indeed the kind of application that Paul might well have written had he applied for a congregation.

Paul was not a well man. All his life he had that thorn in the flesh which so often made life and work a weariness. But how much of the world's work has been done by sick men! Augustus, greatest of the Roman Emperors, suffered from a stomach ulcer, and Julius Caesar, one of the greatest of all the generals, was an epileptic. To the end of the day, Nelson was violently sea-sick every time he put to sea. Sick men have so often written their names across history.

Paul was quite certainly not a handsome man. In the third-century work called *The Acts of Paul and Thecla*, there is a description of Paul which is so unflattering that it must be genuine: "A man of little stature, thin-haired upon the head, crooked in the legs, of good state of body, with eyebrows joining, and nose somewhat hooked." Certainly, from the point of handsome looks, no one would have looked twice at this man Paul.

Still further, it seems that Paul was not even a very good speaker, and that he was certainly no orator. The Corinthians said of him that "his bodily presence is weak, and his speech of no account" (II Corinthians 10.10).

Paul was not alone in this. One of the most crowd-drawing preachers Scotland has ever had was Thomas Chalmers; and they said of him that when he preached he never lifted his head from his manuscript, that he actually followed the line he was reading with his finger as he read, and that he read in a broad Fifeshire accent innocent of any elocutionary attraction.

Paul apparently had none of the gifts—and yet there can have been few preachers in history who were more effective. Where did his effectiveness come from?

It came, I think, from one thing—an unanswerable experience of Jesus Christ. It is told that when the Church at Ecclefechan was looking for a minister, Thomas Carlyle's father, who was an elder there, said simply: "What this kirk wants is a minister who knows Jesus Christ other than at secondhand."

Men were compelled to listen to Paul because it was obvious when Paul spoke that this was no carried story, but something which he knew personally to be true.

Polish and elegance can leave a congregation quite cold; experience and sincerity never fail to move men. In the last analysis, we can never bring to anyone else an experience which we have not had ourselves.

IT'S TIME TO THINK OF EASTER

I have just been hearing about the sudden death of a church organist. He literally dropped dead in his middle forties. He was a man who all his life had lived for music in the service of worship. Even when he was in the army during the war he still found time and opportunity for music in the service of God. In this country he and his padre managed to get a portable harmonium somewhere or other, and toured the search-light batteries holding services; and when the war reached Europe, again and again in Italy, in Greece and in other places, he would find or make the opportunity to make music for worship. This week, as I write, his life came suddenly to an end.

And as it happened, the very day he died he said something which was astonishingly prophetic. It was his custom to co-operate with the organist and choir of a nearby Church to prepare a praise service at the great seasons of the Christian year. And just before he died, he had telephoned the organist of the other Church and had said: "*It's time we were thinking of Easter.*" And so, thinking of Easter and of the life everlasting, his life on earth came suddenly to an end.

It's time that we were thinking of Easter. It is one of the strange things in the modern Church that we think of the Easter faith only at Easter time. It is at Easter time almost alone that we think of the Resurrection and of the life to come; it is at Easter time almost alone that we sing the hymns of the Easter faith. And this is so wrong. I think that we have forgotten the origin of Sunday, the Lord's Day. The Sabbath, the Jewish holy day, commemorated the rest of God after the labour of the six days of creation; the Sunday, the Lord's Day, commemorates the Resurrection of our Lord, for it was on that day that he rose from the dead.

In the early Church the Resurrection was the star in the firmament of the Church. The Resurrection was the one glorious fact on which all worship and all life were founded. To that centrality of the Easter faith, the Resurrection faith, we would do well to return.

It is the Easter faith, the faith in the risen and living Lord, which makes us able to meet life. For if we believe that Jesus Christ is risen and living, then we must believe that all life is lived in his presence, that we are literally never alone, that we are called upon to make no effort, to endure no sorrow, to face no temptation without him.

There is a wonderful unwritten saying of Jesus, a saying which is not in any of the Gospels, but which is surely his: Jesus said: *Wherever they may be they are not without God; and where there is one alone, even then I am with him. Raise the stone and there you will find me; cleave the wood and I am there.* Where the mason works at the stone and where the carpenter works at the wood, Jesus Christ is there. We have only to compare that saying with the saying of a man who did not know Jesus Christ. The ancient preacher wrote: "Who hews stones shall be hurt by them; who cleaves wood is endangered by it" (Ecclesiastes 10.9). For the Christless man, work was a penance and a peril; for the man who knows the risen Christ, work is a sharing of the presence of the risen Lord. "Work," as Jeremias puts it, "is a blessing, because it is hallowed by the presence of Jesus."

And warm, sweet, tender, even yet
A present help is He;
And faith has still its Olivet,
And love its Galilee.

With the Easter faith, with the presence of the risen Lord, life becomes a glory.

It is the Easter faith, the faith in the risen and living Lord, which makes us able to meet death. It is the Easter faith that we have a Friend and a Companion who lived and who died and who is alive for evermore, who is the Conqueror of death. The presence which is with us in life is with us in death and beyond.

A writer tells how his father died. His father was old and ill. One morning the writer tells how he went up to his father's bedroom to waken him. The old man said: "Pull up the blinds so that I can see the morning light." The son pulled up the blind, and even as the light entered the room, the old man sank back on his pillows dead. Death was the coming of the morning light.

It is time that we were thinking of Easter. The Easter faith should be in our thoughts not simply at a certain season of the Christian year; it ought to be the faith in which Christians daily live, and in which they die, only to live again.

ALIVE WHILE YOU LIVE

I have just this morning heard what was to me a new story of that great scholar, preacher and saint, my old teacher, A. J. Gossip.

Gossip lived a very full life when he was occupying his chair in Trinity College and in Glasgow University. When he was just about to retire from teaching, one of his colleagues, thinking of the change that must come, asked him, "What will you do when you retire?" Back came the answer: "What will I do when I retire? Why, man, keep on living till I'm dead!"

And when Gossip said *living*, he meant living with a capital L!

One of the extraordinary things about the Christian experience is the sheer joyous vitality that it brings into life. When D. L. Moody was converted in the shoe-store amidst the shoes, he went out and said: "I thought the old sun shone a good deal brighter than it ever had before—I thought that it was just smiling upon me, and as I walked out upon Boston Common and heard the birds singing in the trees, I thought they were all singing a song to me. Do you know, I fell in love with the birds. I had never cared for them before. It seemed that I was in love with all creation."

The universe was suddenly gloriously and joyously alive.

In due time Wilfred Grenfell of Labrador was converted by Moody. "He started me working for all I was worth," said Grenfell, "and made religion real fun—a new field brimming with opportunities."

Life became real fun when life became Christian.

As George Wade Robinson the hymn-writer has it:

Heaven above is softer blue,
Earth around is sweeter green;
Something lives in every hue,
Christless eyes have never seen:
Birds with gladder songs o'erflow,
Flowers with deeper beauties shine,
Since I know, as now I know,
I am His, and He is mine.

Let us ask: How does this new vital joy enter into life?

When a man becomes a Christian, life becomes *the outward-looking life*. So long as a man thinks of nothing but his own problems, his own sorrows, his own health, his own disappointments, life is a hypochondriacal thing. To have too much time to think about oneself is almost certainly to think oneself into illness. The Christian looks out, and he becomes so concerned with others that he forgets himself.

In Africa, when they have a specially heavy burden to carry, they tie it to one end of a stick, then they tie a stone of equal weight to the other end of the stick, and then they carry the stick and the two burdens across their shoulders. The one balances the other, and two burdens are easier than one. Start carrying someone else's load, and you can forget your own.

When a man becomes a Christian, life becomes *the onward-looking life*. There is a weary sameness about the worldly life, a repetitiveness, a sheer boredom. But the one thing of which the Christian is quite sure is that he is on the way to somewhere. For the Christian life is not a tread-mill but a pilgrimage, so that even, in the wilderness, the Christian journeys towards the sunrise (Numbers 21.12).

When a man becomes a Christian, life becomes an *upward-looking life*. He sees things in the light of eternity, and he sees things in the light of God. And immediately two things happen.

The most ordinary things become important and thrilling, because it is in the performance of them that a man is making or marring a destiny or winning or losing a crown.

The hardest things become easy, because there is nothing that is done alone. An atheist has been described as a man with no invisible means of support, but the Christian has the help and the presence of God in every task and at every time.

Outward, onward, upward—these are the directions of the Christian life, and when one lives looking in these directions, in truth he can go on living until he dies.

CONVERTED—BY COURTESY

One of the most interesting hymns in the Revised Church Hymnary is the hymn of which the first verse runs:

One who is all unfit to count
As scholar in Thy school,
Thou of Thy love hast named a friend—
O kindness wonderful!

The interest of that hymn lies in the fact that it is one of the very few great hymns that the younger churches have yet produced. It is the work of Narayan Vaman Tilak, and was originally composed in Marathi.

The story of Tilak's conversion to Christianity is a very interesting and significant one. He was a well-known Marathi poet before he was converted to Christianity.

One day he was travelling in a train with an Englishman who treated him with the most perfect courtesy, instead of resenting his presence as many a European at that time might well have done. They talked and grew to be friendly. Finally the Englishman gave Tilak a New Testament and urged him to study it. "If you do so," the Englishman said, "you will be a Christian within two years." To Tilak at the moment this seemed a quite impossible prediction.

He had been so impressed by the courtesy of the Englishman that he began to read the New Testament. The book gripped him. "I could not tear myself away," he said, "from these burning words of love and tenderness and truth." Two years later to the day, he was baptised in the Christian Church at Bombay.

Now here is the notable thing. It was, of course, the reading of the New Testament which converted Tilak; but the fact remains true that he would never even have begun to read that book had it not been for the Christian courtesy of the nameless and unknown Englishman whom he met on the train. Christian courtesy converted Tilak.

There is something here which is worth pondering. More than one attitude can be encountered in evangelism.

There is the evangelist who preaches with an unconscious superiority. He utters his condemning tirades against the sinner; he dangles the sinner over the pit of hell; his stock in trade is largely threat and denunciation. He speaks from a height downwards; his whole assumption is that he speaks from a position of safety to those who are in peril.

Evangelism like that is far more likely to produce resentment than response.

There is a kind of pugnacious evangelism. Its attitude is that there is no salvation outside its particular way of thinking, and that any theology which does not think as it thinks is a lie. It is marked by intolerance and by harsh criticism of all those who differ from it. It attempts to bring men to Christ, but it has not itself the spirit of Christ.

The highest and most effective kind of evangelism is marked by the basic quality of sympathy. It does not stand over the sinner; it sits beside the sinner. It does not draw a distinction between itself and the sinner; it identifies itself with the sinner. It speaks as one hell-deserving sinner to another.

"True evangelism", as someone has said, "is one

starving man telling another starving man where he has found bread."

The great High Priest, Jesus Christ himself, is "touched with the feeling of our infirmities" (Hebrews 4.15). It is this gift of sympathy and identification which really draws men to Christ.

One who made confession to him tells of a thing which Studdert Kennedy, Woodbine Willie, said. This persons says: "I want to mention an incident which is very precious to me, and which shows the wonderful understanding he had. I went to the Rector for my first Confession, and among all the sins which I had to confess there was one that made me squirm. But it had to be done, of course. He saw how I felt, and as I finished he said with infinite tenderness: 'Yes, my dear, that's my great temptation, too!' "

Here was one who could sit where the sinner sat.

We wonder sometimes why evangelism is not more effective than it is. So long as it speaks from above, and so long as its accent is threat and condemnation, so long as it speaks with intolerance, and limits the way to God to its way, it is bound to awaken nothing but resistance and resentment. Evangelism must speak with Christian courtesy.

FOR PITY'S SAKE

I have just come back, as I write this, from one of my periodical stays in London Central Y.M.C.A. On this occasion my stay coincided with the Association Dinner, and with their accustomed courtesy and kindness, the officials of the Association invited me to come to the dinner.

One of the two main speakers was the General Secretary, Mr Harry Smith, who has an admirable and enviable gift of saying the most important things in the most memorable way. I cannot refrain from passing on a story which Harry told—with apologies to all civil servants.

There was a civil servant who, at the end of his life, thought that he would like to work on a farm. He went to the farm, and the farmer took him on. His first assignment was to clean out the bull's pen. He did this with no trouble at all, and with no fear of the bull.

His next assignment was to whitewash some of the farm buildings. This he did willingly and happily and efficiently. The next day the farmer was to be away all day, and he wished to give the ex-civil servant a job that would occupy him all day. He took him to the barn where the potatoes were stored, and he told him to divide them into large, medium and small, and in particular to keep apart one certain size to be used as seed potatoes. So the farmer went off and left him.

In the evening the farmer came home. He went to the barn, and found the ex-civil servant walking up and down the barn, wringing his hands and almost in tears. "What's the matter?" the farmer asked. The ex-civil servant answered: "I don't mind cleaning out the bull's pen. I like whitewashing the out-buildings. But *for pity's sake*, don't ask me to make a decision!"

Now this story may well be a slander on civil servants, but it is true of a great many people in this twentieth century. This generation is very unwilling to make decisions.

A kind of creeping paralysis can get into a man, when he can't even decide what train to take, or what to choose from the restaurant menu, or even to get up out of his chair and go to bed. A man can get into a state in which even the smallest decision is something to put off and to avoid.

There are certain things which ought to be a matter of decision. Our job in life should be a matter of decision. One of the tragedies and disasters of life is that for the majority of people this is not true. Their job is not what they chose, but what they more or less drifted into because there was nothing else available. This, of course, is not so true of the professions, but it does tend to be true of the man who cannot enter one of the professions. And this is in large measure the cause of discontent and unrest and even of inefficiency and bad workmanship, for there are few people either settled or efficient in a job in which they are not really interested.

There are difficulties, immense difficulties, perhaps it is quite impossible for everyone, but it is certainly true that life would be a new thing for many people, if they were doing the work that they had chosen to do.

Our acceptance of membership of the Church should be the result of a perfectly definite act of decision. Too often it is no more than a kind of hall-mark of respectability. Too often it is entered upon because a young person has reached a certain age, or because a friend is doing it. And too often, once the decision to enter upon Church membership is taken, the ceremony of reception is formal and unimpressive. The day on which a person decides to enter into full membership of the Church ought to be a day never to be forgotten.

It may be that we are living in days when people do not like decision, when they do not like deep involvement and pledged loyalty. Yet the fact remains, if a person is to find himself in his work, it must be work that he has deliberately decided to undertake. If Church membership is to mean what it ought to mean, it ought to be a deliberate and conscious pledge of loyalty to Jesus Christ, made in such a way that it will be impossible to forget it.

OURSELVES AND GOD

One Sunday, in our house, we sat listening to a television talk. We were all there, including the grandchildren Jill and Karen. The speaker was talking about prayer. Jill did not seem to be paying much attention. She was, in fact, in process of getting a series of rebukes for distracting the attention of those who wanted to listen. She was bouncing about in the background, climbing up the back of the couch and doing all sorts of forbidden things. After all, when you are not yet four, television talks on prayer haven't an awful lot to say to you.

The speaker had just been saying that there are certain things to remember in prayer. "God," said he, "knows far better than we do what is for our good. God is far wiser than we are." And then from the back of the sofa there came Jill's voice: "*And he's bigger, too!*" Jill had been listening after all.

God, said Jill, is a lot bigger than we are. Reinhold Niebuhr used to love to tell a story about something his daughter said when she was a little girl. One day he wanted to go for a walk, and he wanted the little girl to go with him, and she did not want to go. He painted the attractions of a walk in the open air in glowing words to persuade her, and in the end she went. When they got home, he said to her: "Well, wasn't that lovely? Aren't you glad you came?" And she answered: "I had to come. You're bigger than me!" She came because, as she saw it, she was a victim of *force majeure.*

How do we feel about God? What is our attitude to what God sends? It seems to me that you can have three attitudes to what happens in life.

(a) You can accept it just because *God is bigger than you*, and in the last analysis you can't do anything about it anyway, so it is better to accept it and to be done with it.

That was the Stoic point of view. The Stoics believed that everything, every single thing that happened, was according to the will of God. They therefore said that the one thing to learn was to accept everything without complaint. Not to do so was simply to batter your head against the walls of the universe, a painful process which got you nowhere. So they said epigrammatically: "If you can't get what you want, teach yourself to want what you can get." This was the Omar Khayyam attitude:

*'Tis all a Chequer-board of
Nights and days,
Where Destiny with Men for
Pieces plays,
Hither and thither moves,
and mates, and slays,
And one by one back in the
closet lays.*

There are many who have found a certain bleak peace in the thought that it is all fixed anyway. God is bigger than we are; therefore there's no good fighting.

(b) You can accept things because God is *wiser than we are*. This is better, but it is still not the best. We have all known the kind of people who have a passion for arranging the lives of others. They know best and they genuinely think that you ought to accept their guidance. If we could say no more than that God is wiser than we are, there might well be a kind of cold impersonalness in God's dealing with us. We might think of God sitting in a vast superiority arranging people's lives with a kind of intellectual benevolence, meticulously dealing out what is best for us, but regarding us rather as the pieces in a pattern than as persons with hearts that can be touched and feelings that can be hurt.

(c) So we can come to the last attitude; we can accept things because we *know that God is love*. We can know that God does not impose his will on us just because he is bigger than us. God does not impersonally push us around just because he is wiser than us. God loves us, and therefore he seeks not only our good but our happiness. God has the wisdom to know, and the power to do; he is bigger and wiser than we are. But God also has the love to understand; and so he does not move us around like pieces on a board who cannot say no anyway. When we realise that at the heart of things there is love, then we can say, not in resignation, but in joy: "*Thy will be done!*"

THE ONLY PHYSICIAN

Some time ago I was talking to a psychiatrist in one of the greatest mental hospitals in the country. He was talking about his work, and I was talking about mine; he was speaking as a psychiatrist and I was speaking as a minister of the Gospel.

In a way I envied him, for he must often see the evidence of his work in people who are visibly cured in a way that a minister can very seldom experience.

I said this to him: "I suppose that when people leave this hospital they are cured; I suppose they are rid of all their inhibitions and their complexes and their repressions and so on, and that they are new men and women." He looked at me half-smiling. "So you," he said, "are another of these people who believe in psychiatrists?"

I looked at him questioningly. "Well," I said, "I suppose I am."

"Let me tell you something," he said. "All that a psychiatrist can do is to strip a man naked until you get down to the essential man; and, if the essential man is bad stuff, there is nothing he can do about it. That's where you come in."

I don't think he meant literally that that is where *I* or any other minister comes in; I think he meant that is where *Jesus Christ* comes in.

In any illness there are certain steps which must be gone through before a cure is possible.

There must be *diagnosis* by the doctor. The doctor must be able to put his finger on the spot, and to say that this and this is wrong. The most alarming illnesses and those most difficult to deal with are the illnesses when no one can quite discover what is wrong. You cannot even begin to treat an illness until you find out what is wrong.

There must be *acceptance* by the patience. The patient must accept the verdict and the diagnosis of the doctor. If he completely refuses to believe that there is anything wrong, and if he persists in going on as if nothing is wrong, then he cannot be cured.

In these matters the layman is the ignorant man and the doctor is the man who knows; and the verdict of the man who knows must be accepted.

There must come next the *prescribed treatment* by the doctor. The sole purpose of the diagnosis of the trouble is that the treatment which will work a cure must be prescribed. Once again the doctor is the man who knows, and who can say what will cure.

And there must follow *acceptance of the treatment.* If the patient does not accept it, if he refuses to have the operation, if he pours the bottle of medicine down the drain and throws the box of pills out of the window, if he totally disregards the diet prescribed, then he cannot hope for a cure. He must do as he is told—which is not a thing most of us like to do.

But there is something to be added to this. A man is not only a body; he is also a soul, a spirit, a mind. And the state of his mind and soul and spirit can be such as to hinder the prescribed cure, or even to make it totally ineffective. If he is tense with nerves or bitter with resentment, or if he has a dull hopelessness that anything can be done, then very little, possibly nothing, can be done. The spirit, the mind, must be right before the body can be cured.

This is clearly set out in the greatest tribute in Jewish literature to the physician (in Ecclesiasticus 38.1, 16).

> *My son, when you are sick, do not be negligent,*
> *but pray to the Lord and He will heal you . . .*
> *There is a time when success lies*
> *in the hands of the physicians,*
> *for they too will pray for the Lord.*

The whole thought of the passage is that for a complete cure two things are necessary—the best medical treatment, willingly accepted, and the most intense prayer, faithfully offered. When that happens, then the spirit is in a condition for the body to be cured, for then the grace of God co-ordinates with the skill of man, that skill which God himself has given.

But there is, as the great psychiatrist saw, a sickness of the soul which man is helpless to cure. Only the Divine Physician is adequate to deal with that.

A GREAT FAMILY

The Carnegies are one of the great Scottish families connected with Southesk and with Kinnaird. They take their origin from a man called Jocelyn de Ballinhard, who lived as long ago as 1203. Their family motto is *Dread God*, and a great motto it is.

It speaks of *the need for reverence.* "The fear of God," said the Hebrew sage, "is the beginning of wisdom"

(Proverbs 1.7). By *beginning* he may well mean not the thing with which wisdom begins, but the chief thing is wisdom.

The philosophers speak to us of what they call the *numinous*. The numinous is the feeling of awe which comes to every man at some time or other. It is the feeling that we are in the presence of something which comes from beyond this world, the eerie feeling that there is a presence which is mysterious and inexplicable in the world, a presence of something which is "wholly other" than ourselves.

This the philosophers tell us is the raw material of all religion.

It is true that, through Jesus Christ, there has come to us the friendship of God, and that we can come to him with childlike confidence, and in boldness without dread. But there is a familiarity which can breed contempt in a man with an insensitive heart. When we are in God's house, we should behave with reverence, remembering that the place whereon we stand is holy ground. When we are in God's world we should behave with reverence, remembering that the whole world is the Temple of the Spirit of God, and that in him we live and move and have our being.

We must remember that God is Father; but God is also God, and that the way to approach him is on our knees.

It speaks to us of *the need of obedience*. One of the great troubles of life is that we do not take the commands and the demands of God seriously enough. Somehow, although we know them so well, we are often prepared just to ignore them, or to forget them, as if they did not matter very much.

We must remember this. When we disobey God, when we take our own way, we are not so much breaking God's law as we are breaking God's heart.

One of the things which keeps us from doing many a wrong action is simply the fear to hurt those we love. If we remembered how our thoughtlessness and our disobedience hurt the heart of God, then we would fear and dread to disobey him.

It speaks to us of *the secret of courage*. If we really fear God, we will never fear any man.

When they laid John Knox to rest in his grave, the Earl of Morton looked down. "Here lies one," he said, "who feared God so much that he never feared the face of any man."

Really and truly to fear God is to find for ever the secret of courage in the face of man.

There is a craven and a coward fear. There is an abject and a humiliating fear. There is fear of the consequences, fear of the things that men can do, fear of the things that life can do.

That kind of fear has no place in the Christian life.

There is also a cleansing and an antiseptic fear, a fear which is awe, reverence, dread of God. It is not fashionable now to think much of the fear of God; it is much more fashionable to think sentimentally that God is a good fellow and all will be well.

The fear of God is nevertheless the beginning of wisdom—the foundation of reverence, the foundation of obedience, the mainspring of courage.

TOGETHER . . .

I have been reading with great pleasure Dr F. R. Barry's book on the Church and the ministry, *Asking the Right Questions*. One passage in it has reached me as with a blinding flash of illumination. Dr Barry is speaking of the expression of Christian faith and Christian belief.

One of my difficulties in worship has always been that I have never been happy about the repetition of the Creed. It is, of course, part of the service of the Church of England, though not nearly so universally part of the service of the Church of Scotland.

My trouble has always been that there are certain statements in the Creed that I am not prepared to accept, and I have always felt that to repeat them as an act of worship was dishonest. But this is what Dr Barry says: "In saying the creeds we identify ourselves with the total faith and experience of the Church, trusting that, as our Christian life develops, we may grow into fuller understanding of it. No one Christian can apprehend it all: and indeed the original form of the credal statement is '*We believe*' rather than 'I believe'."

To me this is something infinitely worth saying, and remembering. Here, it seems, for years has been my mistake. Although there are parts where I cannot say, "I believe", it is blessedly true that I can say, "We believe".

I can lose my *un*certainty in the certainty of the whole Church, of the whole company of God's worshipping people. It will be a really notable day when as clearly we introduce our credal confessions not by "I believe" but by "*We* believe".

All this is a demonstration of the folly of thinking of oneself only as an individual. As soon as we become Christians, there is a sense in which we cease to be individuals to become members of the great community of Christ.

As we have seen, my own faith may be puny and meagre and inadequate, but when I enter into the Church, I enter into a tradition and a heritage which is far beyond anything I, as an individual, possess. I am no longer under the grim necessity of being unable to go beyond what I believe; I can remember what *we* believe, and I can take comfort in that.

So I can even in my beliefs unite myself with the fellowship of all believers.

It is definitely so in worship. In a book Dr Alan Walker wrote many years ago, entitled *Everybody's Calvary*, he tells of a young minister in a little village chapel. He invited the congregation to wait for a communion service after the ordinary service was ended. Only two waited. So small was the congregation that he thought of cancelling the whole service, but he decided to go on. He followed the ancient ritual, and he came to the passage: " 'Therefore, with angels and archangels and all the company of heaven, we worship and adore thy glorious name.' " He stopped: the wonder of it gripped him. " 'Angels and archangels and all the company of heaven . . .' God forgive me," he said, "I did not know I was in that company."

In worship even when only two or three are gathered together, Jesus Christ is there, and all the company of heaven are present. You will remember how at Dothan, Elisha opened the eyes of his servant so that he might see the unseen host which encompassed them from heaven (II Kings 6.13–17).

When we worship, even with the two or three, we too are compassed about with a mighty cloud of witnesses (Hebrews 12.1).

It is definitely so with the effort which Christian living and Christian service demand. If we think at all, we are bound to think of things as they should be. The difference is daunting, and sometimes we feel our own weakness and helplessness so much that we come to the conclusion that it is hopeless to do anything about it.

Once again, that is the result of thinking as an individual, and not as a community, a Church scattered throughout every nation upon earth, and all time. At the head is Jesus Christ. Nothing is hopeless in such a fellowship, and with such a Leader.

NO "ACT OF GOD"

Recently I was brought face to face with a problem which I often used to meet when I was a parish minister. One whose main task it is to teach does not have to exercise a pastoral ministry in the same sense as a parish minister must. But a short time ago I had to visit a mother who had lost a daughter in most tragic circumstances. The death of the daughter had taken place as a result of an accident which was in any ordinary way impossible. To this day, no one knows just how this accident occurred. It just should not have happened, yet happen it did.

When it was being investigated, a certain phrase

was used by one of the chief investigators, a man with long experience in such matters. He said that the accident was so impossible of explanation that all he could say was that it was "an act of God".

It is difficult to imagine a more terrible and a more blasphemous phrase. What kind of God can people believe in, when they attribute the accidental death of a girl of twenty-four to an act of God? How can anyone who is left possibly pray to a God who would do a thing like that?

During my own parish ministry, I was never able to go into a house where there had been an untimely and tragic death or sorrow and say: "It is the will of God." When a child or a young person dies too soon, when there is a fatal accident, maybe due to someone's mistake or misjudgment, that is not an act of God, neither is it the will of God. It is, in fact, the precise opposite. It is against the will of God, and God is just as grieved about it as we are.

If a terrible and incurable disease strikes someone, if a child is run down and killed by a motor-car, driven maybe by a reckless or a drunken driver, if there is a disaster in the air or at sea or on the railways, that is not the will of God. It is exactly and precisely what God did not will. It is due to some human failure or to some human selfishness.

God gave men free will because there could neither be goodness nor love without free will, and exactly for that reason the action of men can run right counter to the will of God.

I do not think that anyone can calculate the vast amount of damage that has been done by suggesting that terrible and tragic events in life are the will of God.

When Jesus was on this earth in the body, he healed the sick; he raised to life the little daughter of Jairus, and the son of the widow at Nain. Quite clearly, Jesus did not think sickness and illness and untimely death the will of God. Quite clearly, he thought them the reverse of the will of God. They were the very things that he had come to help and to overcome.

What then can we say at a time like this?

We can say that God is as grieved as we are, that he is sharing in our sorrow and our grief, that he is afflicted in all our afflictions, that his heart is going out to meet our hearts.

We can say that he has it in his power to make it up to those who are taken too soon away, and to those to whom sorrow and suffering has tragically come. If God is justice, and if God is love, I am as certain as it is possible to be certain of anything, that there is a life to come. And in that life to come God is seeing to it that the life cut off too soon is getting its chance to blossom and flourish, and the life involved in tragedy is finding its compensation. The eternal world is redressing the balance of the world of time.

We can say that Christianity has never pretended to explain sorrow and suffering. It may often be that in any tragedy there is traceable an element of human fault, human sin; in any disaster the reason may well lie in human error. Yet even when all such cases are taken into account, there remains much that is sheerly inexplicable.

Christianity offers no cheap and facile explanation. In face of such things, we have often to say: "I do not know why this happened." But what Christianity does triumphantly offer is the power to face these things, to bear them, to come through them, and even to transform them so that the tragedy becomes a crown.

When such things happen, let us at least stop blasphemously talking about their being the will of God.

CONTROL FOR TOO LONG

Bishop Lesslie Newbigin has published an excellent and thought-provoking book, *A Faith For this One World.* Very near the beginning of it, he tells us that for the people of Asia "the great new fact of our time is the end of colonialism." We all know that this is the generation in which former colonies are becoming independent nations.

But not long after this, he goes on to quote something else. "In 1957, the Liberian delegate to the United Nations complained that his country suffered as compared with Ghana in not having the advantage of being a colony." Here, indeed, there is something to think about. It is in one sense true that the one aim and end of many people is the end of colonialism; in another sense it is also true that a country which is or was a colony has something very precious.

Now government and parenthood are very closely related; they in fact ought to function under the same principles. So, if we ask the question, "What is it that goes wrong with government, and turns colonialism from being a good thing into a bad thing?" we are not asking a merely academic and political question. We are asking a question the answers to which may well shed a flood of light not only on the conception of Empire, but also on the conception of parenthood.

In the first place, government quite clearly goes wrong when it consciously or unconsciously thinks in terms of exploitation. Any government which regarded its colonies as territories to be exploited for its own profit, is undoubtedly storing up a world of trouble.

Can parenthood be like that? Unfortunately it can. There are parents who desire their children to do well at school, in university, in all kinds of realms in which there is competition, not nearly so much for the sake of the child, as for the credit it will bring to them. There are children who are driven not for the good of the child, but more for the sake of the parent's ego. There are parents who regard their children much as they would regard an insurance policy. They expect their children to look after them and support them in age. Far be it from me to say that a child has no duties to an aged parent. But the parent who is wise will remember that his or her children will one day have a home of their own, and the introduction of someone else into that home, or the demand of support from that home, may well cause problems which come near to defying solution.

No son was ever nearer to his father than I was, and yet my father even after my mother's death, would not live with me—and he was right. There are cases when nothing else is possible, but there are balances in a home which can be tragically, easily upset by the incoming of even a well-loved stranger as a permanent resident.

In the second place, government goes wrong when it does not fit and equip those who are governed to govern themselves. And parental control, the first object of which is not to enable the child to go out and live his own life, can achieve nothing but tragedy.

To return to Lesslie Newbigin—Lesslie Newbigin draws a contrast between the action of the modern Church to the new Churches, and the action of the early Church to the new Churches. When Paul made a missionary journey he set up Churches here and there; he ordained elders; and *he left them to get on with it.* He had to. He paid them visits; but they governed themselves.

The modern Church tends to keep the young Churches on leading strings for scores of years, thinking, it seems, that until the leaders of the younger Churches are trained and educated in Western culture and theology they cannot govern.

I well know that it is not as simple as that; but that is the principle behind it; and Lesslie Newbigin holds it to be wrong, and pleads for a return to the almost recklessly adventurous policy of the early Church.

However that may be, a teacher's duty is to teach a child to think for himself, and a parent's duty is to teach a child to live for himself; and the sooner the better, for there is no more demoralising thing in this world than control exercised too long. In the last analysis, Christianity means having faith in God, and faith also in people.

LEARN, LEARN, LEARN!

Some time ago I had the great pleasure of being at a Conference on Christian Education in St Andrews. It was quite one of the happiest weeks that I have spent for a long time. It had the great advantage of being in St Andrews, Scotland's loveliest university town. We stayed in St Salvator's, one of the finest of its halls. Good talk and discussion was to be had far into the night—and the early morning. There were excursions and tours to the many places of interest in the town and in the countryside, added to social fun in plenty.

All the time there was learning about the Bible, and about the Christian faith, and about the communication of the Bible and the faith in day schools. And to add to the interest, there were people present from America and Jamaica and Australia to tell us of their experience and their work.

But the thing that struck me most of all was this—of the one-hundred-and-eighty people of all ages, and from all kinds of places, practically all teachers—*they had all come to learn.*

They certainly underlined one of life's great truths—no one can teach, unless he is prepared to go on learning all the time.

One of the saddest things I come across is that sometimes when people pass their final examination, or when they receive their degree, or when they get their post, they think their days of learning are ended. I have actually known a student to sell his textbooks the day his college course ended.

To keep on learning, certain things need to be kept in mind.

We need to remember our own ignorance. Quintilian, the Roman teacher of oratory, said of certain of his students: "They would doubtless have been excellent students, if they had not been convinced of their own knowledge." As the old proverb reminds us: "He who knows not, and knows not that he knows not is a fool—avoid him; he who knows not and knows that he knows not is a wise man—seek his company."

We must never think that there is an age at which we stop learning. No one is ever too old to learn. Cato learned Greek at eighty. When Corot, the great painter, was nearly seventy, he said, "If God spares me for another ten years, I think I may still learn to paint"

Once the great actress Marie Tempest acted in a play which was a failure. Her own performance was brilliant, but the play failed and had to be taken off. There was a very sad luncheon party at the end of the play and everyone was very depressed. Suddenly Marie Tempest brightened up. "Everybody," she said, "at the beginning of their career must expect reverses." When she said that, she was sixty-five—and for her it was the beginning. "Age has its opportunities no less than youth."

One of the surest ways to stay young is to stay interested; and the only sure way to stay interested is to go on learning to the end of the day.

We must always be ready to learn about ourselves. The last thing that most of us know is ourselves. It takes humility to know oneself.

Aristippus and Aeschines were two great Greeks who were friends, and Aristippus was a famous philosopher. Anger rose between them. Someone asked Aristippus: "Where now is the friendship of you two?" "It is asleep," came the answer, "but I will waken it." So he went to Aeschines. "Do I appear to you," he asked, "so utterly unfortunate and incurable as not to be able to receive correction from you?" And Aeschines moved by his friend's humility forgot his anger.

It takes humility to say: "Please tell me my faults." It takes humility to ask for criticism, but it is the way to learn about ourselves, and so to grow in grace.

We must always be learning about God. There is a difference between a *childlike* and a *childish* faith; and it is often the tragedy of life that people mature in years in the physical sense, but not in the spiritual sense. Our faith must grow deeper and deeper as the years go on. There is so much of God to know that not all eternity is time enough to know Him.

A happy secret is that of the teachers with whom I spent such a happy week.

GET ON WITH THE JOB!

What would you do, if you were told that you had an incurable illness, and that you were doomed very soon to die? I have been thinking of that question because I have been reading the story of Dr Thomas A. Dooley, in Walter Russell Bowie's book *Men of Fire*.

Thomas A. Dooley as a young doctor straight from medical school, went with the United States Army to Vietnam in 1954. There he saw disease, famine, squalor, death such as he had never seen. In 1956, his service term came to an end, and most men would have thought it escape, but not Thomas A. Dooley. He could not forget. So he went to the Vietnam ambassador in America and volunteered to lead a medical mission to a country in which there was precisely one fully medically trained doctor for two million people. He went because he could not help it, and he worked because he could not help it.

Then quite suddenly he discovered that what he thought had been a harmless tumour on his chest was malignant cancer. So in America he was operated on again. In the hospital he dreamed of a ceremony that he had seen out in the east. The ceremony of the burning of the mountain was carried out every year. Before the monsoon rains, the people burned the mountain because they thought—and rightly—that the ashes fertilised the soil for the planting of the new rice.

He knew what the dream meant. "I knew the meaning of my dream . . . I must, into the burnt soil of my personal mountain, plant the new seedlings of my life. . . . Whatever time was left, whether it was a year or a decade, would be more than just a duration. I would continue to help the clots and clusters of withered and wretched in Asia, to the utmost of my ability. The words of Camus rang through. 'In the midst of winter, I suddenly found that there was in me an invincible summer.' Maybe I could not be tender in a better way."

So the young man doomed to die went back to Vietnam. Round his neck he had a St Christopher medal—Dooley was a Roman Catholic—and on the back of the medal four lines by Robert Frost:

The woods are lovely, dark and deep,
But I have promises to keep,
And miles to go before I sleep,
And miles to go before I sleep.

"If I stop now, I'll probably die sooner," he said. So he went back and worked twenty hours a day, until he literally collapsed at his work.

They brought him back to New York, and on 18th January 1961, Thomas A. Dooley died, one day after his thirty-fourth birthday.

Here was a man whose one motto was: "Get on with the job." It is a good one.

In sorrow—Get on with the job. The work that has been done by men and women with broken hearts is one of the great facts of history.

It was because his young and adored wife died that William Bright plunged into the work that won the repeal of the Corn Laws. It was because her daughter was killed that Josephine Butler engaged in the work which made her one of the greatest social reformers of her generation.

We do not forget our sorrows; we cannot; but to withdraw and to brood is the way to resentment and to nothing but unhappiness. At such a time get a job and get on with it. There is comfort in work.

In disappointment—Get on with the job. There are people who are rather like children who, if they do not get their own way, will not play any more. There are people, who, for some reason or other, have been disappointed in something on which they set their hearts, and from that time they stop doing even what they have been doing. They grow bitter and retire within themselves.

In disappointment, get on with the job. If you can't get the job you want, get on with the job you can get. There is satisfaction in any job well done.

In success—Get on with the job. When you read the New Testament you see at once that the reward for work well done is more work to do (Matt. 25.14–30). There are those who, when they have achieved something, rest on their oars. There is no better way of getting old too quickly. When one job is finished, get on with another job, for that way lies life.

In face of death—Get on with the job. As Stevenson had it, if you know you will never finish your folio, get on with your page. There is no better way for the end to find us than working hard so long as strength lasts.

There are plenty of people in the world who want nothing so much as to dodge the job. The world needs people whose one aim is to get on with the job.

THREEPENCE A TIME

This afternoon I was at a sale of work—a gathering to which I hardly ever go. But it was being held at a friend's church, and he asked me to attend.

There were many interesting things there, but one interested me more than others. In that congregation is a lad who is a Scottish international football player. He is also a Sunday school teacher in that congregation. Now this lad is also a brilliant member of the Scottish football club that won the Scottish Cup. And what do you think he did to help the sale of work?

He succeeded in persuading his club to lend the Scottish Cup—a massive bit of silverware—for display; and at the sale of work the Scottish Cup was put into a room, and for the sum of threepence you could go in and look at it. I think that there is a tremendous lesson for every church member here. This lad wanted to do something to help his church. He must have said to himself: "What is there I can do?" And he found the one thing that he could offer, and he offered it.

Jesus thought the world of people who did that. Once he was away out in a lonely place with a crowd of tired and hungry people. He wanted to give them something to eat before they started on the long tramp home, and he suggested to his disciples that they should do so, and the disciples said it was hopeless to think about it.

But there was a boy there who had his picnic lunch with him—five little rolls and two little fishes like sardines. He knew Jesus was looking for food, and he brought them along and offered them, and a miracle happened (John 6.5-13). And the miracle happened because a boy offered the one thing he had to offer.

It was near the end of Jesus' life and he was in the house of Simon the leper at Bethany, and there was a woman who loved Jesus for what he had done for her. All she had was an alabaster box of ointment, and she came and she anointed him with it. And there were some there who said that this was a foolish and a wasteful thing to do.

But Jesus paid her the biggest compliment you can pay anyone. He said: "Don't worry and criticise her. *She hath done what she could*" (Mark 14.3–9). She offered what she had to offer, and she gave the world a moment of immortal loveliness which will live for ever.

I'm sure you remember the old story of the acrobat who became a Christian. He came into a cathedral and he knelt before a statue of the Virgin Mary. He wanted so much to offer something, but he was poor and he had nothing to give. Then he looked round to see that there was no one watching, and he began to offer all he had to offer—his somersaults, his handstands, his acrobatic tricks.

When he had finished his routine he knelt there, and —the legend says—the Virgin stepped down from her statue and gently wiped the sweat from his brow. He offered what he had to offer.

What a Church we could make it be if people offered what they had to offer. *Jesus does not want what we haven't got; he wants what we have got.* Maybe we have a voice— and there is a church choir which could use it. Maybe we can teach a little—and there is a Sunday school which could use that. Maybe we have some skill or craft—and there's a job on the church buildings to be done which could use that.

We've got a home; and there are lonely people in our town. Jesus could use that home if we offered it to him, and if we were given to hospitality. Maybe there is a new housing area around our church or in our district; it's a big job to visit all these people and to give them an invitation to worship. We've got an evening or two to spare; the church could use that evening for a visit or two.

Maybe we've got a car, and there's an old person who could be doing with a lift to church, who maybe can't get to church any other way. Jesus could use that car.

There is a Scottish international football player who gave his church what he had to offer. What about us doing the same?

HE WILL SUSTAIN THEE

A short time ago I heard a very well known Glasgow minister tell of an incident which he had never forgotten.

More than thirty years ago now he had been at a service conducted by a very famous preacher who for many years had occupied a great pulpit with the greatest distinction. After the service my friend went round to speak to the famous man. "Sir," he said, "when I think of the strain of preaching from this famous pulpit, I do not know how you have carried on all these years." The great preacher answered: "*In this job you do not carry on; you are carried on.*"

My friend went on to say that at the time it had

seemed to him almost a "slick" answer, but the years had taught him that it was nothing but the truth.

The Bible is full of this truth of the support of God. "Cast your burden on the Lord," said the Psalmist, "and he will sustain you" (Psalm 55.22). "When you pass through the waters, I will be with you," Isaiah heard God say, "and through the rivers, they shall not overwhelm you" (Isaiah 43.2). "The eternal God is your dwelling-place," said Moses, "and underneath are the everlasting arms" (Deuteronomy 33.27). Again and again the promise recurs.

There are three things to be said about this.

It is the experience of life that the promise is true. The plain fact is that many of us would bear witness that we have been made able to pass the breaking-point and not to break, that we have been enabled to come through that which we would have said to be impossible, if we had been told in advance that it was to happen.

But this promise is true only upon conditions. The first condition is that we must accept what happens. If we are in a state of bitterness and resentment, then the promise is not for us.

Carlyle dealt roughly with the lady who said: "I accept the universe." "By God," said Carlyle, "she'd better!"

Paul Sangster tells of an incident when his father went to visit a girl in hospital who was going blind, and whom no human skill was able to help. "Mr Sangster," Jessie said, "God is going to take my sight away." For a little while Sangster did not answer. Then he said, "Don't let him, Jessie. Give it to him." "What do you mean?" she asked. "Try to pray this prayer," he answered: " 'Father, if for any reason I must lose my sight, help me to give it to you.' "

You remember Job in the midst of the disasters which smote him: "The Lord gave, and the Lord hath taken away; blessed be the name of the Lord" (Job 1.21).

Before God's promise can come true, we have to accept that which happens to us. This is not to say that all sorrow and suffering and pain and disaster are the will of God. In many cases they are not; they are the result of the sin and the folly and the ignorance of man. But whatever happens, and however it happens, it has to be accepted before it can be transformed.

There is a second condition. We have to try to do our best with, and in, any situation in which we are involved. Acceptance does not mean that we sit down passively and do nothing whatever about a situation. It does not mean that we abandon the struggle to face life with gallantry and with efficiency. It means that what we can do, we will do.

No one ever gets anywhere by running away from life; however difficult life may be we still have to stand up to it. No one ever achieves anything by refusing to help himself.

Suppose health be lost, there is something we can do to pick up the threads again.

Suppose devastating sorrow comes, there is something we can do to get through the terrible days.

Suppose crushing disappointment comes, and hopes are dead, there is something left out of which to rebuild.

Suppose some sin or folly or mistake wrecks life, there is something still left to be salvaged from the wreckage.

It is always true that God helps those who help themselves; and it is also true that God is helpless to help those who refuse to be helped.

When a man faces things in all their agony, God comes in and makes the impossible possible.

A MISTAKE

I have a friend who is an extraordinary man. He is a successful business man, well able to travel to the continent, to France and to Italy, when he wants a holiday. He is an expert naturalist in the things of the district where he lives. And he is also a distinguished poet. He was telling me with great glee about a thing which happened to him during this very week in which I write.

He was coming south from where he stays—a long railway journey. He is not an extravagant man, but, as he said himself, he wanted to think and to compose his mind, so he decided to travel first class on the train.

Now to look at my friend I do not think that you would jump to the conclusion that he possessed all the gifts which he does possess. So he got into a first class railway carriage in which one man was already seated. No sooner had he sat down than the man already in the carriage looked across at him in cold disapproval and said: "Are you aware that this is a first class carriage?"

This man had entirely misjudged my friend, and, looking on the outward man, concluded that he had no right to be in a first class railway carriage.

In a way that story of his is merely amusing. But it is typical of the way in which some people judge other people; they judge entirely by externals. T. E. Lawrence was a quite close friend of Mr and Mrs Thomas Hardy. As everyone knows, T. E. Lawrence laid down his rank in the Army and became an aircraftsman in the RAF.

Sometimes he used to go to tea with Mr and Mrs Hardy at Max Gate, Hardy's house. One day he happened to turn up on the same afternoon as the Mayoress of Dorchester. The lady was affronted; she turned to Mrs Hardy and said in French that in all her born days she had never been asked to sit down to tea with a private soldier—for she had no idea who this aircraftsman was.

There was a deep silence which no one broke, until T. E. Lawrence said courteously: "I beg your pardon, Madame, but can I be of any use as your interpreter? Mrs Hardy knows no French." There followed the very complete collapse of a Lady Mayoress.

There can hardly be anything more dangerous in this world than to judge by externals.

There are those who judge others by their clothes. What would they have said, if they had come across Francis Thompson in the days of his poverty in London, with his coat fastened tight to conceal the fact that he did not possess a shirt, and with his immortal poems, written on old envelopes, in his pockets?

There are those who judge others by their accent. What would they have said, if they had heard Thomas Chalmers preaching in the broadest of broad Scots accents to his Glasgow congregation? They would have fastidiously shut their ears to the flaming truth proclaimed by the uncouth voice.

There are those who judge by worldly success. Maybe they have forgotten the story that Jesus told about the man who was so rich that he did not know what to do with all his possessions, but who, for all that, was a fool (Luke 12.13–21).

There are people who would have looked with

contempt on a little Jewish tent-maker who wandered about Asia Minor with a strange new message; and there are people who would have looked at a carpenter from Nazareth as a person of no importance because he happened to work with his hands.

We may make such a mistake; but God never does. He sees the person behind the externals—and he is never wrong.

TRUE PERSPECTIVE

One of the staggering things about the human mind is how it can lose all sense of proportion. It can magnify trifles until they fill the whole horizon; and it can set side by side things which are of no importance and things which are of eternal importance, and feel no shattering incongruity in the juxtaposition.

Edmund Gosse tells how his father chronicled his birth in his diary. His father was a naturalist; it was a household in which the birth of a child was not really welcomed. When Edmund was born, his father entered in his diary: "E. delivered of a son. Received green swallow from Jamaica." With an astonishing lack of perspective, the birth of a man child into the world, and the arrival of a green swallow from Jamaica are set down side by side.

Mrs Belloc Lowndes in her collection of memories, *A Passing World*, sets down a letter which she wrote to her mother in the autumn of 1914, in the early days of the First World War: "London has become very melancholy. The mourning worn by relatives of the soldiers who have been killed is beginning to show in the streets, and strikes a tragic note. Everything is going to be terribly dear. I got in a case of China tea this morning at the old price, and in the afternoon it went up twopence a pound, so now I wish I had got in two cases."

Here is a woman complaining that the price of China tea is going up twopence a pound when she was moving in a world of broken hearts. The sheer insensitive blindness of a juxtaposition like that is appalling.

We live in a world where people are for ever getting things out of true perspective, a world where one of the rarest of all things is a sense of proportion, a world where people so often seem quite incapable of distinguishing between the things which matter and the things which do not matter.

There is nothing new about this. A man who worked in a paper factory came to see Dr Johnson. He had taken from the factory two or three sheets of paper and some pieces of string to tie up parcels of his own; and by doing so had convinced himself that he had committed a deadly sin. He would not stop talking and lamenting about this trivial business. At last Dr Johnson burst out: "Stop bothering about paper and pack-thread when we are all living together in a world that is bursting with sin and sorrow."

How often friendships are shattered by some trifle! How often the peace of a congregation is wrecked on some completely unimportant detail! How often people delude themselves that they are standing on principles when they are fussing about trifles! How often someone whose heart is breaking is astonished and bewildered at the things which fill other people's lives and talk!

There is only one way to get our perspectives right —and that is to see things in the light of eternity, and in the light of the Cross.

Dr Alan Walker has made that clear to us in the moving story already recounted from his *Everybody's Calvary*, where the young minister suddenly found himself in a larger company altogether than the two with whom he celebrated the communion service when the rest of the congregation had gone. And you and I may do as much—to take upon one's lips those great words of the service: "Therefore with angels and archangels and all the company of heaven . . ." is to move into another dimension. God forgive us, if we never know ourselves in that company!

If we could but see this world against the background of eternity, if we could but see it in the light of the Cross, if we could but see it in the presence of God, or, if that is asking too much, if we could see it simply against the background of human tragedy and human sorrow and broken hearts, we would get back the true perspective.

Trifles should be seen as trifles.

END—AND BEGINNING

Some time ago two things happened very closely to each other which seemed to me very definitely to mark the end of chapters in life. The one was the departure of the Hastings from the editorship of the *Expository Times*, a parting which for me broke a connection which goes back at least a quarter of a century. The other was the death of Sir Hector Hetherington, the former Principal of Glasgow University, without whom it was difficult for my generation to visualise the University at all.

These two events had happened and they were much in my mind. So, thinking of them, I was present at the memorial service for Sir Hector, and before the service I was talking to a distinguished professor who will be retiring from his chair at the end of September. I suppose that the cumulative effect of all this was depressing as far as I was concerned, and I said to the senior professor: "Well, we're at the end of an epoch." He turned and put his hand on my shoulder. "Remember," he said, "if we are at the end of one epoch, we are at the beginning of another."

This was well and bravely spoken, and it seems to me that it was a rebuke to all pessimism and depression.

There are certain things of which that wise saying reminds us.

(a) That our look in life should always be the forward look. It seems to me that we might well define the beginning of old age as the day on which we begin to look back instead of forward. It is the day on which we think rather of what we have done, than of what we still may do.

The backward look is very characteristic of churches and of congregations. There are many congregations suffering from what might be called the handicap of history. At one time or another they had a great period, or rather more probably, a period which memory has wrapped in a golden glow, and they talk for ever of what things used to be like in Mr So-and-So's ministry, and at such-and-such a time. They look back instead of forward, and when that happens the spirit of a congregation is dead. Pray God that to the end of the day we keep the forward look.

(b) It reminds us that any time is a time of opportunity. It is possible to look on the same thing as a disaster, or a challenge. There is a story told of Sir Winston Churchill. There was a time in the early stages of the war when disaster seemed to be imminent. Churchill called a meeting of his leaders. He told them the facts, told them that the nation stood alone, and stood alone with practically no resources other than spirit and courage. It was clear that at that moment some at least of the gathering would have been prepared to give in. There was a moment's silence, and then Churchill said quietly: "Gentlemen, I find it rather inspiring."

To him, the disaster was an opportunity. Any situation is an opportunity for the person who will grasp it.

(c) But the fact that the end of one epoch is the beginning of another also reminds us that there is a time to stop and there is a time to begin. In the Qumran community, from which the famous Dead Sea Scrolls came, there was an interesting law as to the selection of the judges of the community. They were to be skilled in the Book of Study and in the fundamentals of the Covenant. "Their minimum age shall be twenty-five and their maximum age sixty," for men's mental powers recede before they have fulfilled their days (*The Zadokite Document* 10.4–10), on which passage G. Vermes comments that they thus "saved the machinery of government from an encumbrance of aged men."

People keep on too long for two reasons—one is because they want to, and the other is because there is no one willing to take on the work; but if we remember that one epoch ends and another begins, we will also remember that there is a time to lay down work, and there is a time to take it up, and thus we shall neither cling to it too long nor refuse to shoulder the burden in time.

THREE AGES—THREE SINS

June Bingham, in her vivid introduction to the life and thought of Reinhold Niebuhr, *Courage to Change*, quotes a thing that Niebuhr said in 1959, when he was no longer young, and had come through much: "When one is young it is natural to be polemical. As one grows older one wonders whether one is polemical because one has grown in wisdom or because one has diminished in energy."

A saying like that sets one thinking. The danger that threatens life does not remain constant. The temptations which come to us do not remain the same. Each age has its own special sins and faults which are characteristic of it.

The fault of youth is to be in too big a hurry. And very often that haste has a consequence which can be worse than itself. It often means that youth finds it very difficult to take the long view of things.

"Rome was not built in a day", "Hasten slowly", "The more hurry, the less speed"—these are all proverbs, but they were certainly not coined by youth, and they are certainly seldom quoted by youth.

Inevitably youth is a time when feelings are intense and when passions run high. Youth is a time when the moment can be very precious, and when next year can seem a very long way away, and therefore youth is apt to live in the moment and to clutch at the moment.

Youth needs to learn to wait. Many a young minister, for instance, going to a first charge with all the blazing enthusiasm of youth, embarks on a policy of reformation in which this, that and the next thing are changed. The result is, inevitably, trouble, and if he had only waited for a year or two, until people knew him and liked him, he could have done anything he liked with no trouble at all.

Youth needs to learn to look ahead. Things can look very different when we take the long view of them, and the long view is best, for the Christian view is longest of all, for it sees everything *sub specie aeternitatis*, in relation to eternity.

The fault of middle-age is likely to be an over-cautious and even a cowardly prudence. The trouble is that by the time a man is middle-aged he has given hostages to fortune. He has achieved certain standards of living which he would hate to lose. He will therefore often consent to do and to tolerate things because it is dangerous to resist them. The tendency of middle-age is to set security in the highest place. Many a man in middle-age jogs along as he always did simply because he feels that the devil he knows is a lot better than the devil he doesn't know, and he is afraid to change. He feels that he cannot afford the risk of being adventurous. He feels that it is much safer to be a conformist than a non-conformist. He feels that he is much more likely to keep his place and his job if he accepts things than if he protests against them.

The danger of middle-age is that we may well, in our desire for security, lose iife with a capital L.

The fault of age is that it has come to a stage when it

prefers things as they are. Age is a little tired; and age is a little disillusioned. It is sadly true that the only lesson that a great many people have drawn from life is that there are a large number of things which can't be done, and which are not worth trying. Niebuhr overworked until he had a very serious illness. He said afterwards that he ought to have seen the signs and have stopped in time. He felt afterwards that he did not give enough time to the personal needs of his students. "The warning signal should have been when they started apologising for bothering me." Often age is critical of youth for no other reason than that age wants things left alone, because it does not want to be disturbed.

When a man knows a danger he can do something to meet it. Each age in life has its own danger. We do well to seek ever in our lives *the renewing and recreating grace which is sufficient for all things and for all ages.*

TO THE LAST MINUTE

When I was a parish minister, I had in my congregation an old lady I used to visit almost every week in life. She had been bed-ridden for so long. She was a character, and she spoke the braid Scots tongue and was not ashamed of it. She was a gallant soul, and I am sure that the visits I paid did me more good than they did her. A visit to her room was the best cure for self-pity that I ever came across.

I didn't wear a clerical collar, except for official occasions, and so the old lady seldom saw me dressed in clerical attire. But one day I came to visit her directly after officiating at a funeral. I came upstairs to her room and put my head round the door. She took one look at me, and said peremptorily: "Get awa' oot o' here and change your collar. Ah'm no' decin' yet!"

From her that was a jest, for she loved her Lord and lived daily with him. But I have never quite forgotten it. For so many people that kind of thing is not a jest, but the truth. There are so many people who leave religion and God out of the reckoning till the last minute.

Their general theory is that they can do without the Church, and without prayer, and without God, until they are up against it. So long as life goes smoothly on, they think that they do not need to bother about God. It is only when life falls in, and when the chill breath of death comes near them that they think about God at all.

Shakespeare knew men. In the first act of *The Tempest* he draws the picture of the storm at sea; and when shipwreck is imminent, he has the grim stage direction, "Enter mariners, wet", and their first cry is, "All lost! to prayers, to prayers! All lost!" It was only when all was lost that they turned to prayers.

In *Henry V*, Shakespeare has the immortal scene when the hostess of the tavern and Pistol, Nym and Bardolph talk of the death of Falstaff (ii 3): "'A parted even just between twelve and one, even at the turning o' the tide; for after I saw him fumble with the sheets and play with the flowers and smile upon his fingers' ends, I knew that there was but one way: for his nose was as sharp as a pen, and 'a babbled of green fields. 'How now, Sir John?' quoth I: 'What man! be a good cheer.' So 'a cried out 'God, God, God!' three or four times: now I, to comfort him, bid him 'a should not think of God; I hoped there was no need to trouble himself with any such thoughts yet."

No need to trouble himself yet with thoughts of God—so many people are like that. As Paul had it: It's time to wake out of sleep; your salvation is coming nearer and nearer; the night is far spent, and the day is at hand (Rom. 13. 11–12).

I think it is Dr Frank Boreham who tells of meeting a doctor friend, and, seeing that the doctor was much depressed, Boreham asked what the matter was. The answer he got was: "I have just come from a man for whom I can do nothing; and if he had come to me months ago, when he felt the first twinges of the thing that will kill him, I could have cured him quite easily. But he has let it go too far."

As someone has put it, the trouble is that so many people connect religion with the ambulance corps and not the firing line of life. And it is disastrously easy to put off too long the calling of the ambulance. The Bible is full of the thought that things must be done *while yet there is time.*

And when we come to think of it, is this any way to treat God? Must we forget about him until we need him? Is God someone of whom we only make use? Is God a life-belt or a friend? Surely he should be the friend of every step of the way, and not only the one whom we call in an emergency. The trouble is that when we treat God that way, it is to a stranger that we appeal.

There was an old saint who spent much time in prayer. Someone asked why he spent so much. He answered: "I talk to God every day so that when the desperate moment comes, he will know my voice."

It is always folly to leave things to the last minute.

BEYOND DIFFERENCES

Lately there came to my house a parcel. I opened it and found therein a book and a letter. The book was a gift from the author who wrote it, and the letter was a gracious and kindly word saying that the writer was grateful for certain things of mine that he had read.

In the letter there was one sentence which greatly moved me: "Naturally I come across things at times, which by reason of my own personal convictions (or it may be prejudice through up-bringing!) I find it difficult to accept. But such differences of outlook on critical questions only enhance in my mind the greater fellowship in those things where we are one."

I suppose if you wished to label this gracious friend whom I have never met, you would call him a fundamentalist. I suppose, if you wished to label me, you would call me a liberal. And yet in the things that matter we are one.

Why can't life always be like that? Why is it that we must make *so much* of our differences and *so little* of our agreements? Why is it that we find it so difficult to appreciate things which differ from our own point of view?

In the *Diary* of Sir Walter Scott there is a story. There were two famous Scotsmen who had quarrelled with each other, John Leyden and Thomas Campbell. Scott repeated Campbell's famous *Hohenlinden* to Leyden. Leyden said: "Dash it, man, tell the fellow that I hate him:—but, dash him, he has written the finest verses that have been published these fifty years."

Scott took that queer message to Campbell and Campbell said: "Tell Leyden that I detest him, but I know the value of his critical approbation." Here were two men, hot-tempered enough to quarrel, but big enough to see the greatness in each other.

I wish that theologians and church people were more like that. I wish that one could differ with a man without branding him as a heretic and a sinner and an outsider. After all, it is bound to happen that one should think differently, and should use different methods and different ways, and why not?

I shouldn't think that Tyson (a fast bowler) thinks Wardle (a spin bowler) a heretic because he believes that the best way to remove opposing batsmen (American readers, for "bowler" read "pitcher") is to bowl at them at eighty-seven miles per hour, while Wardle holds that slow bowling is the thing. I should think it entirely probable that Wardle would heartily agree that there are certain kinds of wickets on which Tyson is much more likely to get men out than he is. They have their methods, and they have their common object, and they both belong to the one team.

There are certain things on which we church people differ.

(a) It is the tragedy of the Church that we cannot sit at the Lord's Table together.

J. B. Phillips in *Appointment with God* protests against the apparent desire by any Church to "corner" the mystery of the sacrament. He writes: "I, for one, cannot see by what right I exclude my fellow-Christian from communion with our common Lord." Who are we to shut any man out from him who said: "Him that cometh unto me I will in no wise cast out"?

(b) It is the tragedy of the Church that we have our liturgical wrangles.

One man insists on a prayer-book service; another insists on free prayer. One man prays extemporaneously; another regards read prayers as an abomination before the Lord. Surely things like that do not matter. Surely it matters not that worship be the elaborate worship of a cathedral or the bare simplicity of a little meeting-house, *so long as men get to God through it.*

We do not compel everyone to eat the same kind of food for their bodies. Why should we compel them to nourish their spirits with the same kind of prayer?

(c) In some ways most bitter of all is the fight about the Bible, the argument between the fundamentalist and the liberal. Though a change is coming.

One man condemns to outer darkness anyone who says that Moses did not write the Pentateuch, that the story of Jonah is not literally true, that maybe John the Apostle was not the pen-man of the Fourth Gospel. Another has arrogant contempt for what he regards as academic ignorance.

If only we were a little more sympathetic to each other, if only we would stop labelling each other heretic and outcast, truth would be better served, and the day be nearer when there will be one flock and one shepherd.

FOUR VEILS

Dr John Oman, in his *Vision and Authority*, said that in the human situation there were necessary veils which hid the mystery of God from the eyes of men, the veils of ignorance, of sin, of weakness, and of evanescence. But he goes on to add, to our wonder, that in Christ and in Christianity these four veils are taken away.

The passage runs as follows:

"Enshrouded by these four veils man stands before the mystery of God. By four great Christian doctrines they are taken away. The veil of our ignorance is removed by the Incarnation, the veil of our sin by the Atonement, the veil of our weakness by Grace, the veil of our evanescence by Immortality."

In a sense, here is the whole pith of Christianity.

The Incarnation takes away our ignorance of God.

Long ago Plato said that it was impossible to find out anything about God, and, if by any chance one did find out anything, it was impossible to tell anyone else.

The very essence of Jesus Christ is that in him we see what God is like. Jesus is the Word (John 1.14). The simplest definition of a word is that it is the expression of a thought; in Jesus we see perfectly expressed the thought of God. "He who has seen me," said Jesus, "has seen the Father" (John 14.9). To see Jesus is to see God.

It is true that in Jesus we do not see the great metaphysical attributes of God, like omnipotence and omniscience and omnipresence. Jesus could stagger under the weight of the Cross; there were things that he did not know; he was confined to one place at one time in the days of his flesh. But in Jesus we do see fully and perfectly expressed the attitude of God to men—and that attitude is love.

When we look at Jesus and see how he treated men and women of all sorts and conditions, we can say: "This is how God feels to me."

The Atonement takes away the barrier of sin.

The Church very wisely has never had one official and orthodox theory of the Atonement. But every theory says one thing, although the different theories may say it in different ways. Through the life and death of Jesus Christ, the relationship between man and God was completely and totally changed.

Because of what Jesus Christ is, and what he did, and does, the fear and the estrangement and the distance and the terror are gone. We know that even to us the friendship of God is open. Now that we know what God is like, we can go to him with childlike confidence and boldness.

The gift of Grace removes our helplessness.

When we know what Grace means, more than one precious thing emerges clearly. We know that our relationship to God depends not on our merits, but on his love. We know that he loves us not because of what we are, but because of what he himself is. We know that we are no longer left to face and fight life alone, but that there is open to us all the power and strength of God.

What the ancient world longed for, as Seneca said, was a hand let down to lift us up. And that is precisely what Grace is. It is the hand of God to lift us out of frustration into victory, out of helplessness into power, out of defeat into triumph.

In Grace there is release from the tension of unavailing effort.

The gift of Immortality removes the evanescence of humanity. Jesus, through his glorious gospel, brought life and immortality to light (II Timothy 1.10). We know ourselves now to be on the way, not to death, but to life. We know that death is not the end, but the beginning of life. We know ourselves to be not the children of a moment, but the pilgrims of eternity. And life has a new value, because it is on the way not to extinction and obliteration, but to consummation and to completion.

So left to ourselves, we are bound to live a life in which the inevitable veils of humanity conceal God from us; but in Jesus Christ the veils are removed, and we see God face to face, knowing him as he is, rejoicing in our new-found friendship with him, triumphant in the power in which our weakness becomes his strength, certain that after life here there is a still greater life, both for us and for those whom we love.

Yasmina Reza

Le Dieu du carnage

Présentation, notes, questions et après-texte établis par

SYLVIE COLY

professeure de Lettres

MAGNARD

Sommaire

Après-texte

YASMINA REZA

Yasmina Reza est un écrivain français, née en 1959, dont les œuvres théâtrales et romanesques sont jouées et traduites dans le monde entier.

Les œuvres théâtrales de Yasmina Reza, que l'on peut qualifier de tragédies drôles, sont traduites dans plus de 35 langues et jouées à travers le monde dans des centaines de productions aussi diverses que la Royal Shakespeare Company, le théâtre de l'Almeida, le Berliner ou la Schaubühne à Berlin, le Burgteater de Vienne, ainsi que dans les théâtres les plus renommés du monde entier, de Moscou à Broadway. Elle a obtenu les deux prix anglo-saxons les plus prestigieux : le Laurence Olivier Award (UK) et le Tony Award (USA) pour *« Art »* et *Le Dieu du Carnage*.

Pour le théâtre, elle a publié *Conversations après un enterrement*, *La Traversée de l'hiver*, *L'Homme du Hasard*, *« Art »*, *Trois versions de la vie*, *Une pièce espagnole*, *Le Dieu du carnage*, *Comment vous racontez la partie*, *Bella Figura*.

Le Dieu du carnage a été créé en 2007 par Jurgen Gösch à la Schauspielhaus de Zürich, puis au Berliner Ensemble. La pièce a ensuite été jouée en France, au théâtre Antoine, dans une mise en scène de l'auteur, avec notamment Isabelle Huppert. La pièce est actuellement jouée dans le monde entier et a été adaptée au cinéma par Roman Polanski ; pour ce film, *Carnage*,

Yasmina Reza a obtenu le César du meilleur scénario pour son adaptation de la pièce.

Yasmina Reza est également romancière ; elle a notamment écrit les romans *Hammerklavier*, *Une désolation*, *Adam Haberberg*, *Dans la luge d'Arthur Schopenhauer*, *Nulle part*, *L'Aube*, *Le soir ou la nuit*. *Heureux les heureux*, publié en janvier 2013, a obtenu le prix du journal *Le Monde*. Son dernier roman, *Babylone*, est sorti en septembre 2016 et a obtenu le prix Renaudot. Tous ses romans sont traduits dans de nombreux pays.

Sa pièce *Bella Figura*, a été créée à la Schaubühne de Berlin par Thomas Ostermeier en mai 2015. Yasmina Reza signe la mise en scène en France (création au théâtre Liberté à Toulon en janvier 2017, en tournée, puis au Théâtre du Rond-Point à Paris en novembre 2017).

Elle est montée sur les planches en septembre 2018 au Quai-Théâtre d'Angers, puis à la Scala-Paris, et a joué dans *Dans la luge d'Arthur Schopenhauer*, mise en scène par Frédéric Bélier-Garcia, avec André Marco, Jérôme Deschamps et Christèle Tual.

Yasmina Reza va mettre en scène son dernier texte, *Anne-Marie La Beauté*, au Théâtre National de la Colline en mars 2020.

Elle a également réalisé en 2010 son premier film, *Chicas*.

Yasmina Reza

Le Dieu du carnage

VÉRONIQUE HOULLIÉ.

MICHEL HOULLIÉ.

ANNETTE REILLE.

ALAIN REILLE.

(Entre quarante et cinquante ans.)

Un salon.
Pas de réalisme.
Pas d'éléments inutiles.

Les Houllié et les Reille, assis face à face.
On doit sentir d'emblée qu'on est chez les Houllié et que les deux couples viennent de faire connaissance.

Au centre, une table basse, couverte de livres d'art.
5 *Deux gros bouquets de tulipes dans des pots.*

Règne une atmosphère grave, cordiale[1] *et tolérante.*

VÉRONIQUE. Donc notre déclaration… Vous ferez la vôtre de votre côté… « Le 3 novembre, à dix-sept heures trente, au square de l'Aspirant-Dunant, à la suite d'une altercation ver-
10 bale[2], Ferdinand Reille, onze ans, armé d'un bâton, a frappé au visage notre fils Bruno Houllié. Les conséquences de cet acte sont, outre la tuméfaction[3] de la lèvre supérieure, une brisure des deux incisives, avec atteinte du nerf de l'incisive droite. »

ALAIN. Armé ?

15 VÉRONIQUE. Armé ? Vous n'aimez pas « armé », qu'est-ce qu'on met Michel, muni, doté, muni d'un bâton, ça va ?

ALAIN. Muni oui.

MICHEL. Muni d'un bâton.

VÉRONIQUE *(corrigeant)*. Muni. L'ironie est que nous avons
20 toujours considéré le square de l'Aspirant-Dunant comme un havre de sécurité[4], contrairement au parc Montsouris.

---

1. Polie, ouverte.
2. Dispute, querelle.
3. Gonflement.
4. Refuge sûr.

MICHEL. Oui, c'est vrai. Nous avons toujours dit le parc Montsouris non, le square de l'Aspirant-Dunant oui.

VÉRONIQUE. Comme quoi. En tout cas nous vous remercions 25 d'être venus. On ne gagne rien à s'installer dans une logique passionnelle[1].

ANNETTE. C'est nous qui vous remercions. C'est nous.

VÉRONIQUE. Je ne crois pas qu'on ait à se dire merci. Par chance il existe encore un art de vivre ensemble, non ?

30 ALAIN. Que les enfants ne semblent pas avoir intégré. Enfin je veux dire le nôtre !

ANNETTE. Oui, le nôtre !... Et qu'est-ce qui va arriver à la dent dont le nerf est touché ?...

VÉRONIQUE. Alors on ne sait pas. On est réservé sur le pro- 35 nostic[2]. Apparemment le nerf n'est pas complètement exposé.

MICHEL. Il n'y a qu'un point qui est exposé.

VÉRONIQUE. Oui. Il y a une partie qui est exposée[3] et une partie qui est encore protégée. Par conséquent, pour le moment, on ne dévitalise[4] pas.

40 MICHEL. On essaie de donner une chance à la dent.

VÉRONIQUE. Ce serait quand même mieux d'éviter l'obturation canalaire[5].

ANNETTE. Oui...

---

1. Où les émotions et les sentiments sont plus forts que la raison.
2. Dont on ne connaît pas vraiment les séquelles, les conséquences.
3. Blessée.
4. On ne retire pas le nerf, ce qui ôterait la vie à la dent.
5. Terme de chirurgie dentaire qui consiste à poser un pansement sur une dent malade ou traumatisée.

VÉRONIQUE. Donc il y a une période de suivi où on donne
45 une chance au nerf pour récupérer.

MICHEL. En attendant, il va avoir des facettes en céramique[1].

VÉRONIQUE. De toute façon, on ne peut pas mettre de prothèse[2] avant dix-huit ans.

MICHEL. Non.

50 VÉRONIQUE. Les prothèses définitives ne sont mises en place que lorsque la croissance est terminée.

ANNETTE. Bien sûr. J'espère que… J'espère que tout se passera bien.

VÉRONIQUE. Espérons.

55 *Léger flottement*[3].

ANNETTE. Elles sont ravissantes ces tulipes.

VÉRONIQUE. C'est le petit fleuriste du marché Mouton-Duvernet. Vous voyez, celui qui est tout en haut.

ANNETTE. Ah oui.

60 VÉRONIQUE. Elles arrivent tous les matins directement de Hollande, dix euros la brassée de cinquante.

ANNETTE. Ah bon !

VÉRONIQUE. Vous voyez, celui qui est tout en haut.

ANNETTE. Oui, oui.

---

1. Petites plaques que le dentiste colle sur les dents pour améliorer l'esthétique.
2. Fausses dents.
3. Silence. Le sujet de conversation précédent est épuisé et les convives n'ont pas encore entamé le suivant.

65 VÉRONIQUE. Vous savez qu'il ne voulait pas dénoncer Ferdinand.

MICHEL. Non il ne voulait pas.

VÉRONIQUE. C'était impressionnant de voir cet enfant qui n'avait plus de visage, plus de dents et qui refusait de parler.

70 ANNETTE. J'imagine.

MICHEL. Il ne voulait pas le dénoncer aussi par crainte de passer pour un rapporteur devant ses camarades, il faut être honnête Véronique, il n'y avait pas que de la bravoure[1].

VÉRONIQUE. Certes, mais la bravoure c'est aussi un esprit 75 collectif.

ANNETTE. Naturellement… Et comment… ? Enfin je veux dire comment avez-vous obtenu le nom de Ferdinand ?…

VÉRONIQUE. Parce que nous avons expliqué à Bruno qu'il ne rendait pas service à cet enfant en le protégeant.

80 MICHEL. Nous lui avons dit si cet enfant pense qu'il peut continuer à taper sans être inquiété, pourquoi veux-tu qu'il s'arrête ?

VÉRONIQUE. Nous lui avons dit si nous étions les parents de ce garçon, nous voudrions absolument être informés.

85 ANNETTE. Bien sûr.

ALAIN. Oui… *(son portable vibre).* Excusez-moi… *(il s'écarte du groupe ; pendant qu'il parle, il sort un quotidien de sa poche.)*… Oui, Maurice, merci de me rappeler. Bon, dans *Les Échos* de ce matin, je vous le lis… : « Selon une étude publiée dans la revue

---

1. Grand courage.

90 britannique *Lancet* et reprise hier dans le *F.T.*, deux chercheurs australiens auraient mis au jour les effets neurologiques de l'Antril, antihypertenseur[1] des laboratoires Verenz-Pharma, allant de la baisse d'audition à l'ataxie[2]. »… Mais qui fait la veille média[3] chez vous ?… Oui c'est très emmerdant… Non, mais 95 moi ce qui m'emmerde c'est l'A.G.O., vous avez une assemblée générale dans quinze jours. Vous avez provisionné ce litige[4] ?… OK… Et, Maurice, Maurice, demandez au dircom[5] s'il y a d'autres reprises… À tout de suite. *(Il raccroche.)*… Excusez-moi.

MICHEL. Vous êtes…

100 ALAIN. Avocat.

ANNETTE. Et vous ?

MICHEL. Moi je suis grossiste en articles ménagers, Véronique est écrivain, et travaille à mi-temps dans une librairie d'art et d'histoire.

105 ANNETTE. Écrivain ?

VÉRONIQUE. J'ai participé à un ouvrage collectif sur la civilisation sabéenne[6], à partir des fouilles reprises à la fin du conflit entre l'Éthiopie et l'Érythrée. Et à présent, je sors en janvier un livre sur la tragédie du Darfour[7].

---

1. Qui lutte contre l'hypertension artérielle, c'est-à-dire une trop forte pression du sang.
2. Atteinte du système nerveux provoquant le désordre des mouvements.
3. Surveillance de la presse télévisuelle, radiophonique, papier et Internet.
4. Donné des crédits financiers pour régler le problème et payé les avocats.
5. Abréviation des milieux d'affaires pour désigner le directeur commercial d'une société.
6. Civilisation d'Arabie (800 avant J.-C.) dont la figure emblématique est la reine de Saba.
7. Région du Soudan, en Afrique, où la guerre civile particulièrement meurtrière reposant sur un conflit ethnique fait rage depuis 2003.

110 ANNETTE. Vous êtes spécialiste de l'Afrique.

VÉRONIQUE. Je m'intéresse à cette partie du monde.

ANNETTE. Vous avez d'autres enfants ?

VÉRONIQUE. Bruno a une sœur de neuf ans, Camille. Qui est fâchée avec son père parce que son père s'est débarrassé du hamster cette nuit. 115

ANNETTE. Vous vous êtes débarrassé du hamster ?

MICHEL. Oui. Ce hamster fait un bruit épouvantable la nuit. Ce sont des êtres qui dorment le jour. Bruno souffrait, il était exaspéré par le bruit du hamster. Moi, pour dire la vérité, ça faisait longtemps que j'avais envie de m'en débarrasser, je me suis dit ça suffit, je l'ai pris, je l'ai mis dans la rue. Je croyais que ces animaux aimaient les caniveaux, les égouts, pas du tout, il était pétrifié[1] sur le trottoir. En fait, ce ne sont ni des animaux domestiques, ni des animaux sauvages, je ne sais pas où est leur milieu naturel. Fous-les dans une clairière, ils sont malheureux aussi. Je ne sais pas où on peut les mettre. 120 125

ANNETTE. Vous l'avez laissé dehors ?

VÉRONIQUE. Il l'a laissé, et il a voulu faire croire à Camille qu'il s'était enfui. Sauf qu'elle ne l'a pas cru.

130 ALAIN. Et ce matin, le hamster avait disparu ?

MICHEL. Disparu.

VÉRONIQUE. Et vous, vous êtes dans quelle branche ?

ANNETTE. Je suis conseillère en gestion de patrimoine.

VÉRONIQUE. Est-ce qu'on pourrait imaginer… pardonnez-

---

1. Immobilisé par la peur.

135 moi de poser la question de façon directe, que Ferdinand présente ses excuses à Bruno ?

ALAIN. Ce serait bien qu'ils se parlent.

ANNETTE. Il faut qu'il s'excuse Alain. Il faut qu'il lui dise qu'il est désolé.

140 ALAIN. Oui, oui. Sûrement.

VÉRONIQUE. Mais est-ce qu'il est désolé ?

ALAIN. Il se rend compte de son geste. Il n'en connaissait pas la portée. Il a onze ans.

VÉRONIQUE. À onze ans on n'est plus un bébé.

145 MICHEL. On n'est pas non plus un adulte ! On ne vous a rien proposé, café, thé, est-ce qu'il reste du clafoutis Véro ? Un clafoutis exceptionnel !

ALAIN. Un café serré je veux bien.

ANNETTE. Un verre d'eau.

150 MICHEL *(à Véronique qui va sortir)*. Espresso pour moi aussi chérie, et apporte le clafoutis. *(Après un flottement.)* Moi je dis toujours, on est un tas de terre glaise[1] et de ça il faut faire quelque chose. Peut-être que ça ne prendra forme qu'à la fin. Est-ce qu'on sait ?

155 ANNETTE. Mmm.

MICHEL. Vous devez goûter le clafoutis. Ce n'est pas du tout évident un bon clafoutis.

ANNETTE. C'est vrai.

---

1. Allusion au golem de Prague : selon une légende de la tradition juive, un rabbin aurait façonné un homme dans la terre glaise, et la créature se serait animée grâce au souffle de vie.

ALAIN. Vous vendez quoi ?

160 MICHEL. De la quincaillerie d'ameublement. Serrures, poignées de porte, cuivre à souder, et des articles de ménage, casseroles, poêles…

ALAIN. Ça marche ça ?

MICHEL. Vous savez, nous on n'a jamais connu les années d'euphorie[1], quand on a commencé c'était déjà dur. Mais si je pars tous les matins avec mon cartable et mon catalogue, ça marche. On n'est pas comme dans le textile, à la merci des saisons. Quoique la terrine à foie gras, je la vends mieux en décembre !

ALAIN. Oui…

170 ANNETTE. Quand vous avez vu que le hamster était pétrifié, pourquoi ne l'avez-vous pas ramené à la maison ?

MICHEL. Parce que je ne pouvais pas le prendre dans mes mains.

ANNETTE. Vous l'aviez bien mis sur le trottoir.

175 MICHEL. Je l'ai apporté dans sa boîte et je l'ai renversé. Je ne peux pas toucher ces bêtes.

Véronique revient avec un plateau. Boissons et clafoutis.

VÉRONIQUE. Je ne sais pas qui a mis le clafoutis dans le frigo. Monica met tout dans le frigo, il n'y a rien à faire.

180 Qu'est-ce qu'il vous dit Ferdinand ? Sucre ?

ALAIN. Non, non. À quoi il est votre clafoutis ?

---

1. Les années de bonheur ; ici, période de prospérité économique.

VÉRONIQUE. Pommes et poires.

ANNETTE. Pommes et poires ?

VÉRONIQUE. Ma petite recette *(elle coupe le clafoutis et sert des*
185 *parts)*. Il va être trop froid, c'est dommage.

ANNETTE. Pommes poires, c'est la première fois.

VÉRONIQUE. Pommes poires c'est classique mais il y a un truc.

ANNETTE. Ah bon ?

VÉRONIQUE. Il faut que la poire soit plus épaisse que la
190 pomme. Parce que la poire cuit plus vite que la pomme.

ANNETTE. Ah voilà.

MICHEL. Mais elle ne dit pas le vrai secret.

VÉRONIQUE. Laisse-les goûter.

ALAIN. Très bon. Très bon.

195 ANNETTE. Succulent.

VÉRONIQUE. … Des miettes de pain d'épice !

ANNETTE. Bravo.

VÉRONIQUE. Un aménagement du clafoutis picard. Pour être honnête, je le tiens de sa mère.

200 ALAIN. Pain d'épice, délicieux… Au moins ça nous permet de découvrir une recette.

VÉRONIQUE. J'aurais préféré que mon fils ne perde pas deux dents à cette occasion.

ALAIN. Bien sûr, c'est ce que je voulais dire !

205 ANNETTE. Tu l'exprimes curieusement.

ALAIN. Pas du tout, je… *(le portable vibre, il regarde l'écran)*… Je suis obligé de prendre… Oui Maurice… Ah non, pas de

droit de réponse[1], vous allez alimenter la polémique[2]… Est-ce que ça a été provisionné ?… Mm, mm… C'est quoi ces
210 troubles, c'est quoi l'ataxie ?… Et à dose normale ?… On le sait depuis quand ?… Et depuis ce temps-là vous ne l'avez pas retiré ?… Qu'est-ce que ça fait en chiffre d'affaires ?… Ah oui. Je comprends… D'accord *(il raccroche et compose aussitôt un autre numéro, tout en dévorant le clafoutis).*

215 ANNETTE. Alain, sois un peu avec nous s'il te plaît.

ALAIN. Oui, oui, j'arrive… *(portable)* Serge ?… Ils connaissent les risques depuis deux ans… Un rapport interne mais aucun effet indésirable n'est formellement établi… Non, aucune mesure de précaution, ils n'ont pas provisionné, pas un
220 mot dans le rapport annuel… Marche ébrieuse[3], problèmes d'équilibre, en gros tu as l'air bourré en permanence… *(il rit avec son collaborateur)*… Chiffre d'affaires, cent cinquante millions de dollars… Nier en bloc… Il voulait qu'on fasse un droit de réponse cet abruti. On ne va certainement pas faire un droit
225 de réponse, par contre s'il y a des reprises on peut faire un communiqué genre c'est de l'intox à quinze jours de l'A.G.O… Il doit me rappeler… OK *(il raccroche)*… En fait j'ai à peine eu le temps de déjeuner.

MICHEL. Servez-vous, servez-vous.

230 ALAIN. Merci. J'exagère. On disait quoi ?

---

1. Débat, controverse, dispute écrite.
2. Vocabulaire juridique : droit d'une personne ou d'une entreprise de s'exprimer publiquement.
3. Démarche d'une personne ivre.

VÉRONIQUE. Qu'il aurait été plus agréable de se rencontrer en d'autres circonstances.

ALAIN. Ah oui bien sûr.

Donc ce clafoutis, c'est votre mère ?

235 MICHEL. C'est une recette de ma mère mais c'est Véro qui l'a fait.

VÉRONIQUE. Ta mère ne mélange pas les poires et les pommes !

MICHEL. Non.

240 VÉRONIQUE. Elle va se faire opérer la pauvre.

ANNETTE. Ah bon ? De quoi ?

VÉRONIQUE. Du genou.

MICHEL. On va lui mettre une prothèse rotatoire en métal et polyéthylène[1]. Elle se demande ce qui va en rester quand elle 245 se fera incinérer[2].

VÉRONIQUE. Tu es méchant.

MICHEL. Elle ne veut pas être enterrée avec mon père. Elle veut être incinérée et placée à côté de sa mère qui est toute seule dans le Midi. Deux urnes qui vont discuter face à la mer. Ha, ha !...

250 *Flottement souriant.*

ANNETTE. Nous sommes très touchés par votre générosité,

---

1. Genou artificiel.

2. Réduire le corps du défunt en cendres. Les cendres sont ensuite placées dans une urne funéraire.

nous sommes sensibles au fait que vous tentiez d'aplanir cette situation au lieu de l'envenimer[1].

VÉRONIQUE. Franchement c'est la moindre des choses.

255 MICHEL. Oui !

ANNETTE. Non, non. Combien de parents prennent fait et cause pour leurs enfants de façon elle-même infantile[2]. Si Bruno avait cassé deux dents à Ferdinand, est-ce qu'on n'aurait pas eu Alain et moi une réaction plus épidermique[3] ? Je ne suis

260 pas sûre qu'on aurait fait preuve d'une telle largeur de vues.

MICHEL. Mais si !

ALAIN. Elle a raison. Pas sûr.

MICHEL. Si. Parce que nous savons tous très bien que l'inverse aurait pu arriver.

265 *Flottement.*

VÉRONIQUE. Et Ferdinand qu'est-ce qu'il dit ? Comment il vit la situation ?

ANNETTE. Il ne parle pas beaucoup. Il est désemparé[4] je crois.

VÉRONIQUE. Il réalise qu'il a défiguré son camarade ?

270 ALAIN. Non. Non, il ne réalise pas qu'il a défiguré son camarade.

ANNETTE. Mais pourquoi tu dis ça ? Ferdinand réalise bien sûr !

---

1. Tâcher de trouver un terrain d'entente au lieu d'aggraver le conflit.
2. Puéril, comme le ferait un enfant.
3. Instinctive, irréfléchie.
4. Ne sachant plus quoi faire.

ALAIN. Il réalise qu'il a eu un comportement brutal, il ne réalise pas qu'il a défiguré son camarade.

275 VÉRONIQUE. Vous n'aimez pas le mot, mais le mot est malheureusement juste.

ALAIN. Mon fils n'a pas défiguré votre fils.

VÉRONIQUE. Votre fils a défiguré notre fils. Revenez ici à cinq heures, vous verrez sa bouche et ses dents.

280 MICHEL. Momentanément défiguré.

ALAIN. Sa bouche va dégonfler, quant à ses dents, s'il faut l'emmener chez le meilleur dentiste, je suis prêt à participer…

MICHEL. Les assurances sont là pour ça. Nous, nous voudrions que les garçons se réconcilient et que ce genre d'épisode 285 ne se reproduise pas.

ANNETTE. Organisons une rencontre.

MICHEL. Oui. Voilà.

VÉRONIQUE. En notre présence ?

ALAIN. Ils n'ont pas besoin d'être coachés. Laissons-les entre 290 hommes.

ANNETTE. Entre hommes Alain, c'est ridicule. Cela dit, on n'a peut-être pas besoin d'être là. Ce serait mieux si on n'était pas là, non ?

VÉRONIQUE. La question n'est pas qu'on soit là ou pas. La 295 question est souhaitent-ils se parler, souhaitent-ils s'expliquer ?

MICHEL. Bruno le souhaite.

VÉRONIQUE. Mais Ferdinand ?

ANNETTE. On ne va pas lui demander son avis.

VÉRONIQUE. Il faut que ça vienne de lui.

300 ANNETTE. Ferdinand se comporte comme un voyou, on ne s'intéresse pas à ses états d'âme.

VÉRONIQUE. Si Ferdinand rencontre Bruno dans le cadre d'une obligation punitive, je ne vois pas ce qu'il peut en résulter de positif.

305 ALAIN. Madame, notre fils est un sauvage. Espérer de lui une contrition[1] spontanée est irréel. Bon, je suis désolé, je dois retourner au cabinet. Annette, tu restes, vous me raconterez ce que vous avez décidé, de toute façon je ne sers à rien. La femme pense il faut l'homme, il faut le père, comme si ça servait à 310 quelque chose. L'homme est un paquet qu'on traîne donc il est décalé et maladroit, ah vous voyez un bout de métro aérien, c'est marrant !

ANNETTE. Je suis confuse mais je ne peux pas m'attarder non plus… Mon mari n'a jamais été un père à poussette !…

315 VÉRONIQUE. C'est dommage. C'est merveilleux de promener un enfant. Ça passe si vite. Toi Michel, tu appréciais de prendre soin des enfants et tu conduisais la poussette avec joie.

MICHEL. Oui, oui.

VÉRONIQUE. Alors qu'est-ce qu'on décide ?

320 ANNETTE. Est-ce que vous pourriez passer à la maison vers dix-neuf heures trente avec Bruno ?

VÉRONIQUE. Dix-neuf heures trente ?… Qu'est-ce que tu en penses, Michel ?

MICHEL. Moi… Si je peux me permettre…

---

1. Un regret d'avoir mal agi (vocabulaire religieux).

325 ANNETTE. Allez-y.

MICHEL. Je pense que c'est plutôt Ferdinand qui devrait venir.

VÉRONIQUE. Oui, je suis d'accord.

MICHEL. Ce n'est pas à la victime de se déplacer.

VÉRONIQUE. C'est vrai.

330 ALAIN. À dix-neuf heures trente je ne peux être nulle part moi.

ANNETTE. Nous n'avons pas besoin de toi puisque tu ne sers à rien.

VÉRONIQUE. Quand même, ce serait bien que son père soit là.

335 ALAIN *(portable vibre)*. Oui mais alors pas ce soir, allô ?… Le bilan ne fait état de rien. Mais le risque n'est pas formellement établi. Il n'y a pas de preuve… *(il raccroche)*.

VÉRONIQUE. Demain ?

ALAIN. Demain je suis à La Haye.

340 VÉRONIQUE. Vous travaillez à La Haye ?

ALAIN. J'ai une affaire devant la Cour pénale internationale.

ANNETTE. L'essentiel c'est que les enfants se parlent. Je vais accompagner Ferdinand chez vous à dix-neuf heures trente et on va les laisser s'expliquer. Non ? Vous n'avez pas l'air 345 convaincus.

VÉRONIQUE. Si Ferdinand n'est pas responsabilisé, ils vont se regarder en chiens de faïence[1] et ce sera une catastrophe.

ALAIN. Que voulez-vous dire madame ? Que veut dire responsabilisé ?

---

1. Se regarder sans rien se dire.

350 VÉRONIQUE. Votre fils n'est sûrement pas un sauvage.

ANNETTE. Ferdinand n'est pas du tout un sauvage.

ALAIN. Si.

ANNETTE. Alain c'est idiot, pourquoi dire une chose pareille ?

ALAIN. C'est un sauvage.

355 MICHEL. Comment il explique son geste ?

ANNETTE. Il ne veut pas en parler.

VÉRONIQUE. Il faudrait qu'il en parle.

ALAIN. Madame, il faudrait beaucoup de choses. Il faudrait qu'il vienne, il faudrait qu'il en parle, il faudrait qu'il regrette, 360 vous avez visiblement des compétences qui nous font défaut, nous allons nous améliorer mais entre-temps soyez indulgente.

MICHEL. Allez, allez ! On ne va pas se quitter bêtement là-dessus !

365 VÉRONIQUE. Je parle pour lui, je parle pour Ferdinand.

ALAIN. J'avais bien compris.

ANNETTE. Asseyons-nous encore deux minutes.

MICHEL. Encore un petit café ?

ALAIN. Un café d'accord.

370 ANNETTE. Moi aussi alors. Merci.

MICHEL. Laisse Véro, j'y vais.

Flottement.

Annette déplace délicatement quelques-uns des nombreux livres d'art disposés sur la table basse.

375 ANNETTE. Vous êtes très amateur de peinture je vois.

VÉRONIQUE. De peinture. De photo. C'est un peu mon métier.

ANNETTE. J'adore Bacon aussi.

VÉRONIQUE. Ah oui, Bacon.

380 ANNETTE *(tournant les pages)*… Cruauté et splendeur.

VÉRONIQUE. Chaos. Équilibre.

ANNETTE. Oui…

VÉRONIQUE. Ferdinand s'intéresse à l'art ?

ANNETTE. Pas autant qu'il le faudrait… Vos enfants oui ?

385 VÉRONIQUE. On essaie. On essaie de compenser le déficit scolaire[1] en la matière.

ANNETTE. Oui…

VÉRONIQUE. On essaie de les faire lire. De les emmener aux concerts, aux expositions. Nous avons la faiblesse de croire aux 390 pouvoirs pacificateurs de la culture[2] !

ANNETTE. Vous avez raison…

Retour de Michel avec les cafés.

MICHEL. Le clafoutis est-il un gâteau ou une tarte ? Question sérieuse. Je pensais dans la cuisine, pourquoi la Linzertorte[3] 395 est-elle une tarte ? Allez-y, allez-y, on ne va pas laisser cette tranchette.

---

1. Manque de l'école en matière d'éducation artistique.
2. Idée selon laquelle la culture aide à être non-violent.
3. Tarte aux fruits rouges d'origine autrichienne recouverte de fines bandes de pâte croisées.

VÉRONIQUE. Le clafoutis est un gâteau. La pâte n'est pas abaissée mais mêlée aux fruits.

ALAIN. Vous êtes une vraie cuisinière.

400 VÉRONIQUE. J'aime ça. La cuisine il faut aimer ça. De mon point de vue, seule la tarte classique, c'est-à-dire pâte aplatie, mérite le nom de tarte.

MICHEL. Et vous, vous avez d'autres enfants ?

ALAIN. J'ai un fils d'un premier mariage.

405 MICHEL. Je me demandais, bien que ce soit sans importance, quel était le motif de la dispute. Bruno est resté complètement muet sur ce point.

ANNETTE. Bruno a refusé de faire rentrer Ferdinand dans sa bande.

410 VÉRONIQUE. Bruno a une bande ?

ALAIN. Et il l'a traité de « balance ».

VÉRONIQUE. Tu savais que Bruno avait une bande ?

MICHEL. Non. Je suis fou de joie.

VÉRONIQUE. Pourquoi tu es fou de joie ?

415 MICHEL. Parce que moi aussi j'étais chef de bande.

ALAIN. Moi aussi.

VÉRONIQUE. Ça consiste en quoi ?

MICHEL. Tu as cinq, six gars qui t'aiment et qui sont prêts à se sacrifier pour toi. Comme dans *Ivanhoé*[1].

---

1. Roman de Walter Scott datant de 1819. Ivanhoé est un chevalier qui fédère ses troupes par sa bravoure et sa fidélité et se bat aux côtés de Richard Cœur de Lion et Robin des Bois.

420 ALAIN. Comme dans *Ivanhoé*, exactement !

VÉRONIQUE. Qui connaît *Ivanhoé* aujourd'hui ?

ALAIN. Ils prennent un autre type. Un Spiderman.

VÉRONIQUE. Enfin je constate que vous en savez plus que nous. Ferdinand n'est pas resté aussi muet que vous voulez bien 425 le dire. Et pourquoi il l'a traité de « balance » ? Non, c'est bête, c'est bête comme question. D'abord je m'en fiche, et ce n'est pas le sujet.

ANNETTE. On ne peut pas rentrer dans ces querelles d'enfant.

VÉRONIQUE. Ça ne nous regarde pas.

430 ANNETTE. Non.

VÉRONIQUE. En revanche ce qui nous regarde, c'est ce qui s'est passé malheureusement. La violence nous regarde.

MICHEL. Quand j'étais chef de bande, en septième, j'avais battu en combat singulier Didier Leglu, qui était plus fort que 435 moi.

VÉRONIQUE. Qu'est-ce que tu veux dire Michel ? Ça n'a rien à voir.

MICHEL. Non, non, ça n'a rien à voir.

VÉRONIQUE. On ne parle pas d'un combat singulier. Les 440 enfants ne se sont pas battus.

MICHEL. Tout à fait, tout à fait. J'évoquais juste un souvenir.

ALAIN. Il n'y a pas une grande différence.

VÉRONIQUE. Ah si. Permettez-moi monsieur, il y a une différence.

445 MICHEL. Il y a une différence.

ALAIN. Laquelle ?

MICHEL. Avec Didier Leglu, nous étions d'accord pour nous battre.

ALAIN. Vous l'avez amoché ?

450 MICHEL. Sûrement un peu.

VÉRONIQUE. Bon, oublions Didier Leglu. Est-ce que vous m'autorisez à parler à Ferdinand ?

ANNETTE. Mais bien sûr !

VÉRONIQUE. Je ne voudrais pas le faire sans votre accord.

455 ANNETTE. Parlez-lui. Il n'y a rien de plus normal.

ALAIN. Bonne chance.

ANNETTE. Arrête Alain. Je ne comprends pas.

ALAIN. Madame est animée…

VÉRONIQUE. Véronique. On va mieux s'en sortir si on ne 460 s'appelle plus madame et monsieur.

ALAIN. Véronique, vous êtes mue par une ambition pédagogique, qui est sympathique…

VÉRONIQUE. Si vous ne voulez pas que je lui parle, je ne lui parle pas.

465 ALAIN. Mais parlez-lui, sermonnez-le, faites ce que vous voulez.

VÉRONIQUE. Je ne comprends pas que vous ne soyez pas davantage concerné.

ALAIN. Madame…

470 MICHEL. Véronique.

ALAIN. Véronique, je suis on ne peut plus concerné. Mon fils blesse un autre enfant…

VÉRONIQUE. Volontairement.

ALAIN. Vous voyez, c'est ce genre de remarque qui me raidit.
475 Volontairement, nous le savons.

VÉRONIQUE. Mais c'est toute la différence.

ALAIN. La différence entre quoi et quoi ? On ne parle pas d'autre chose. Notre fils a pris un bâton et a tapé le vôtre. On est là pour ça, non ?

480 ANNETTE. C'est stérile.

MICHEL. Oui, elle a raison, ce genre de discussion est stérile.

ALAIN. Pourquoi éprouvez-vous le besoin de glisser « volontairement » ? Quel type de leçon je suis censé recevoir ?

ANNETTE. Écoutez, nous sommes sur une pente ridicule,
485 mon mari est angoissé par d'autres affaires, je reviens ce soir avec Ferdinand et on va laisser les choses se régler naturellement.

ALAIN. Je ne suis aucunement angoissé.

ANNETTE. Eh bien moi je le suis.

490 MICHEL. Nous n'avons aucune raison d'être angoissés.

ANNETTE. Si.

ALAIN *(portable vibre)*. … Vous ne répondez pas… Aucun commentaire… Mais non, vous ne le retirez pas ! Si vous le retirez, vous êtes responsable… Retirer l'Antril, c'est reconnaître
495 votre responsabilité ! Il n'y a rien dans les comptes annuels. Si vous voulez être poursuivi pour faux bilan et être débarqué dans quinze jours, retirez-le de la vente…

VÉRONIQUE. À la fête du collège, l'an dernier, c'était Ferdinand qui jouait Monsieur de… ?

500 ANNETTE. Monsieur de Pourceaugnac[1].

VÉRONIQUE. Monsieur de Pourceaugnac.

ALAIN. Les victimes on y pensera après l'assemblée Maurice… On verra après l'assemblée en fonction du cours…

VÉRONIQUE. Il était formidable.

505 ANNETTE. Oui…

ALAIN. On ne vas pas retirer le médicament parce qu'il y a trois types qui marchent de traviole !… Vous ne répondez à rien pour le moment… Oui. À tout de suite… *(coupe et appelle son collaborateur).*

510 VÉRONIQUE. On se souvient bien de lui dans *Monsieur de Pourceaugnac.* Tu t'en souviens, Michel ?

MICHEL. Oui, oui…

VÉRONIQUE. Déguisé en femme, il était drôle.

ANNETTE. Oui…

515 ALAIN *(au collaborateur).* … Ils s'affolent, ils ont les radios aux fesses, tu fais préparer un communiqué qui ne soit pas du tout un truc défensif, au contraire, vous y allez au canon, vous insistez sur le fait que Verenz-Pharma est victime d'une tentative de déstabilisation à quinze jours de son assemblée générale, 520 d'où vient cette étude, pourquoi elle tombe du ciel maintenant, etc. Pas un mot sur le problème de santé, une seule question : qui est derrière l'étude ?… Bien *(raccroche).*

Court flottement.

---

1. Personnage principal de la pièce éponyme de Molière.

MICHEL. Ils sont terribles ces labos. Profit, profit.

525 ALAIN. Vous n'êtes pas censé partager ma conversation.

MICHEL. Vous n'êtes pas obligé de l'avoir devant moi.

ALAIN. Si. Je suis tout à fait obligé de l'avoir ici. Contre mon gré, croyez bien.

MICHEL. Ils te fourguent leur camelote sans aucun état d'âme.

530 ALAIN. Dans le domaine thérapeutique[1], toute avancée est associée à un bénéfice et à un risque.

MICHEL. Oui, j'entends bien. N'empêche. Vous faites un drôle de métier quand même.

ALAIN. C'est-à-dire ?

535 VÉRONIQUE. Michel, ça ne nous regarde pas.

MICHEL. Un drôle de métier.

ALAIN. Et vous, vous faites quoi ?

MICHEL. Moi je fais un métier ordinaire.

ALAIN. C'est quoi un métier ordinaire ?

540 MICHEL. Je vends des casseroles je vous l'ai dit.

ALAIN. Et des poignées de porte.

MICHEL. Et des mécanismes de WC. Des tas d'autres choses encore.

ALAIN. Ah des mécanismes de WC. J'aime bien ça. Ça
545 m'intéresse.

ANNETTE. Alain.

ALAIN. Ça m'intéresse. Le mécanisme de WC m'intéresse.

---

1. Dans le domaine de l'industrie des soins médicaux.

MICHEL. Pourquoi pas.
ALAIN. Vous en avez combien de sortes ?
550 MICHEL. Il y a deux systèmes. À poussoir ou à tirette.
ALAIN. Ah oui.
MICHEL. Ça dépend de l'alimentation.
ALAIN. Eh oui.
MICHEL. Soit l'arrivée d'eau se fait par le haut soit elle se fait
555 par le bas.
ALAIN. Oui.
MICHEL. Je peux vous présenter un de mes magasiniers, qui est spécialiste, si vous voulez. Mais il faudra vous déplacer à Saint-Denis-La Plaine.
560 ALAIN. Vous avez l'air très compétent.
VÉRONIQUE. Est-ce que vous comptez sanctionner Ferdinand d'une manière ou d'une autre ? Vous continuerez la plomberie dans un environnement plus adéquat.
ANNETTE. Je ne me sens pas bien.
565 VÉRONIQUE. Qu'est-ce que vous avez ?
ALAIN. Ah oui tu es pâle chérie.
MICHEL. Vous êtes pâlotte, c'est vrai.
ANNETTE. J'ai mal au cœur.
VÉRONIQUE. Mal au cœur ?… J'ai du Primpéran…
570 ANNETTE. Non, non… Ça va aller…
VÉRONIQUE. Qu'est-ce qu'on pourrait… ? Du Coca. Du Coca c'est très bon *(elle part aussitôt en chercher).*
ANNETTE. Ça va aller…
MICHEL. Marchez un peu. Faites quelques pas.

575 *Elle fait quelques pas.*
Véronique revient avec le Coca-Cola.

ANNETTE. Vous croyez ?...
VÉRONIQUE. Oui, oui. À petites gorgées.
ANNETTE. Merci...
580 ALAIN *(il a rappelé discrètement son bureau)*. ... Passez-moi Serge s'il vous plaît... Ah bon... Qu'il me rappelle, qu'il me rappelle tout de suite... *(raccroche)*. C'est bon le Coca ? C'est bon pour la diarrhée plutôt ?
VÉRONIQUE. Pas uniquement *(à Annette)*. Ça va ?
585 ANNETTE. Ça va... Madame, si nous souhaitons réprimander notre enfant, nous le faisons à notre façon et sans avoir de comptes à rendre.
MICHEL. Absolument.
VÉRONIQUE. Absolument quoi Michel ?
590 MICHEL. Ils font ce qu'ils veulent avec leur fils, ils sont libres.
VÉRONIQUE. Je ne trouve pas.
MICHEL. Tu ne trouves pas quoi Véro ?
VÉRONIQUE. Qu'ils soient libres.
ALAIN. Tiens. Développez *(portable vibre)*. Ah pardon... *(Au*
595 *collaborateur)*. Parfait... Mais n'oublie pas, rien n'est prouvé, il n'y a aucune certitude... Vous gourez pas, si on se loupe là-dessus, Maurice saute dans quinze jours et nous avec.
ANNETTE. Ça suffit Alain ! Ça suffit maintenant ce portable ! Sois avec nous merde !

hang up

600 ALAIN. Oui… Tu me rappelles pour me lire *(raccroche)*. Qu'est-ce qui te prend, tu es folle de crier comme ça ! Serge a tout entendu !

ANNETTE. Tant mieux ! Ça fait chier ce portable tout le temps !

ALAIN. Écoute Annette, je suis déjà bien gentil d'être ici…

605 VÉRONIQUE. C'est extravagant.

ANNETTE. Je vais vomir.

ALAIN. Mais non tu ne vas pas vomir.

ANNETTE. Si…

MICHEL. Vous voulez aller aux toilettes ?

610 ANNETTE *(à Alain)*. Personne ne t'oblige à rester…

VÉRONIQUE. Non, personne ne l'oblige à rester.

ANNETTE. Ça tourne…

ALAIN. Regarde un point fixe. Regarde un point fixe toutou.

ANNETTE. Va-t'en, laisse-moi.

615 VÉRONIQUE. Il vaudrait mieux qu'elle aille aux toilettes quand même.

ALAIN. Va aux toilettes. Va aux toilettes si tu vas vomir.

MICHEL. Donne-lui du Primpéran.

ALAIN. Ça ne peut pas être le clafoutis quand même ?

620 VÉRONIQUE. Il est d'hier !

ANNETTE *(à Alain)*. Ne me touche pas !…

ALAIN. Calme-toi toutou.

MICHEL. S'il vous plaît, pourquoi s'échauffer bêtement !

ANNETTE. Pour mon mari, tout ce qui est maison, école, 625 jardin est de mon ressort.

ALAIN. Mais non !

ANNETTE. Si. Et je te comprends. C'est mortel tout ça. C'est mortel.

VÉRONIQUE. Si c'est tellement mortel pourquoi mettre des
630 enfants au monde ?

MICHEL. Peut-être que Ferdinand ressent ce désintérêt.

ANNETTE. Quel désintérêt ?!

MICHEL. Vous le dites vous-même…

Annette vomit violemment.
635 *Une gerbe brutale et catastrophique qu'Alain reçoit pour partie.*
Les livres d'art sur la table basse sont également éclaboussés.

MICHEL. Va chercher une bassine, va chercher une bassine !

Véronique court chercher une bassine tandis que Michel lui tend le plateau des cafés au cas où.
640 *Annette a un nouveau haut-le-cœur mais rien ne sort.*

ALAIN. Tu aurais dû aller aux toilettes toutou, c'est absurde !

MICHEL. C'est vrai que le costume a écopé !

Très vite, Véronique revient avec une cuvette et un torchon.
On donne la cuvette à Annette.

645 VÉRONIQUE. Ça ne peut pas être le clafoutis, c'est sûr que non.

MICHEL. Ce n'est pas le clafoutis, c'est nerveux. C'est nerveux ça.

VÉRONIQUE *(à Alain)*. Vous voulez vous nettoyer dans la salle de bains ? Oh là là, le Kokoschka[1] ! Mon Dieu !

650 *Annette vomit de la bile dans la cuvette.*

MICHEL. Donne-lui du Primpéran.

VÉRONIQUE. Pas tout de suite, elle ne peut rien ingurgiter là.

ALAIN. C'est où la salle de bains ?

VÉRONIQUE. Je vous montre.

655 *Véronique et Alain sortent.*

MICHEL. C'est nerveux. C'est une crise nerveuse. Vous êtes une maman Annette. Que vous le vouliez ou non. Je comprends que vous soyez angoissée.

ANNETTE. Mmm.

660 MICHEL. Moi je dis, on ne peut pas dominer ce qui nous domine.

ANNETTE. Mmm…

MICHEL. Chez moi, ça se met dans les cervicales. Blocage des cervicales.

665 ANNETTE. Mmm… *(encore un peu de bile)*.

VÉRONIQUE *(revenant avec une autre cuvette dans laquelle il y a une éponge)*. Qu'est-ce qu'on va faire avec le Kokoschka ?

---

1. Écrivain et peintre expressionniste autrichien. Ici, métonymie désignant un livre d'art sur ce peintre.

MICHEL. Moi j'assainirais avec du Monsieur Propre… Le problème c'est le séchage… Ou alors tu nettoies à l'eau et tu mets 670 un peu de parfum.

VÉRONIQUE. Du parfum ?

MICHEL. Mets mon *Kouros*, je ne l'utilise jamais.

VÉRONIQUE. Ça va gondoler.

MICHEL. On peut donner un coup de séchoir et aplatir avec 675 d'autres livres par-dessus. Ou repasser comme avec les billets.

VÉRONIQUE. Oh là là…

ANNETTE. Je vous le rachèterai…

VÉRONIQUE. Il est introuvable ! Il est épuisé depuis longtemps !

ANNETTE. Je suis navrée…

680 MICHEL. On va le récupérer. Laisse-moi faire Véro.

Elle lui tend la cuvette d'eau et l'éponge avec dégoût. Michel entreprend de nettoyer l'ouvrage.

VÉRONIQUE. C'est une réédition qui a plus de vingt ans du catalogue de l'exposition de 53 à Londres !…

685 MICHEL. Va chercher le séchoir. Et le *Kouros*. Dans le placard des serviettes.

VÉRONIQUE. Son mari est dans la salle de bains.

MICHEL. Il n'est pas à poil ! *(Elle sort tandis qu'il continue de nettoyer.)*… J'ai enlevé le gros. Un petit coup sur les Dolganes… 690 Je reviens.

Il sort avec sa cuvette sale.

Véronique et Michel reviennent presque ensemble.
Elle avec le flacon de parfum, lui avec une cuvette d'eau propre.
Michel termine son nettoyage.

695 VÉRONIQUE *(à Annette)*. Ça va mieux ?
ANNETTE. Oui.
VÉRONIQUE. Je pulvérise ?
MICHEL. Où est le séchoir ?
VÉRONIQUE. Il l'apporte dès qu'il a fini.
700 MICHEL. On l'attend. On mettra le *Kouros* au dernier moment.
ANNETTE. Je pourrais utiliser la salle de bains moi aussi ?
VÉRONIQUE. Oui, oui. Oui, oui. Bien sûr.
ANNETTE. Je ne sais pas comment m'excuser…

705 *Elle l'accompagne et revient aussitôt.*

VÉRONIQUE. Quel cauchemar atroce !
MICHEL. Lui, faudrait pas qu'il me pousse trop.
VÉRONIQUE. Elle est épouvantable elle aussi.
MICHEL. Moins.
710 VÉRONIQUE. Elle est fausse.
MICHEL. Elle me gêne moins.
VÉRONIQUE. Ils sont épouvantables tous les deux. Pourquoi tu te mets de leur côté ? *(Elle pulvérise les tulipes.)*
MICHEL. Je ne me mets pas de leur côté, qu'est-ce que ça veut
715 dire ?

VÉRONIQUE. Tu temporises, tu veux ménager la chèvre et le chou.

MICHEL. Pas du tout!

VÉRONIQUE. Si. Tu racontes tes exploits de chef de bande, tu
720 dis qu'ils sont libres de faire ce qu'ils veulent avec leur fils alors que le gosse est un danger public, quand un gosse est un danger public c'est l'affaire de tout le monde, c'est dément qu'elle ait dégueulé sur mes livres! *(Elle pulvérise le Kokoschka.)*

MICHEL *(indiquant).* Les Dolgans[1]...

725 VÉRONIQUE. Quand on sent qu'on va gerber, on prend les devants.

MICHEL. ... Le Foujita[1].

VÉRONIQUE *(elle pulvérise tout).* C'est dégueulasse.

MICHEL. J'étais limite avec les mécanismes de chiottes.

730 VÉRONIQUE. Tu étais parfait.

MICHEL. J'ai bien répondu, non?

VÉRONIQUE. Parfait. Le magasinier était parfait.

MICHEL. Quel merdeux. Comment il l'appelle?!...

VÉRONIQUE. Toutou.

735 MICHEL. Ah oui, toutou!

VÉRONIQUE. Toutou! *(Ils rient tous les deux.)*

ALAIN *(revenant, séchoir à la main).* Oui, je l'appelle toutou.

VÉRONIQUE. Oh... Pardon, ce n'était pas méchant... On se moque facilement des petits noms des autres! Et nous, com-
740 ment on s'appelle Michel? Sûrement pire?

---

1. **Peuple sibérien nomade. Ici, désigne par métonymie un livre d'art sur le sujet.**
2. **Désigne par métonymie le livre *de*, ou *sur*, Tsuguharu Foujita, artiste français d'origine japonaise.**

ALAIN. Vous vouliez le séchoir ?

VÉRONIQUE. Merci.

MICHEL. Merci *(s'emparant du séchoir)*. Nous on s'appelle darjeeling, comme le thé. À mon avis c'est nettement plus ridicule !

745 *Michel branche l'appareil et entreprend de sécher les livres. Véronique aplatit les feuilles mouillées.*

MICHEL. Lisse bien, lisse bien.

VÉRONIQUE *(par-dessus le bruit et tandis qu'elle lisse)*. Comment se sent-elle la pauvre, mieux ?

750 ALAIN. Mieux.

VÉRONIQUE. J'ai très mal réagi, j'ai honte.

ALAIN. Mais non.

VÉRONIQUE. Je l'ai accablée avec mon catalogue, je n'en reviens pas.

755 MICHEL. Tourne la page. Tends-la, tends-la bien.

ALAIN. Vous allez la déchirer.

VÉRONIQUE. C'est vrai… Ça suffit Michel, c'est sec. On tient absurdement à des choses, on ne sait même pas pourquoi au fond.

760 *Michel referme le catalogue qu'ils recouvrent tous deux d'un petit monticule de gros livres.*

Michel sèche le Foujita, les Dolgans, etc.

MICHEL. Et voilà ! Impec.

Et d'où ça vient toutou ?

765 ALAIN. D'une chanson de Paolo Conte qui fait wa, wa, wa.

MICHEL. Je la connais ! Je la connais ! *(Chantonne.)* Wa, wa, wa !... Toutou ! Ha ! ha !... Et nous c'est une variation de darling, après un voyage de noces en Inde. C'est con !

VÉRONIQUE. Je ne devrais pas aller la voir ?

770 MICHEL. Vas-y darjeeling.

VÉRONIQUE. J'y vais ?... *(retour d'Annette)*... Oh Annette ! Je m'inquiétais... Vous êtes mieux ?

ANNETTE. Je crois.

ALAIN. Si tu n'es pas sûre, tiens-toi loin de la table basse.

775 ANNETTE. J'ai laissé la serviette dans la baignoire, je ne savais pas où la mettre.

VÉRONIQUE. Idéal.

ANNETTE. Vous avez pu nettoyer. Je suis désolée.

MICHEL. Tout est parfait. Tout est en ordre.

780 VÉRONIQUE. Annette, excusez-moi, je ne me suis pour ainsi dire pas occupée de vous. Je me suis focalisée sur mon Kokoschka...

ANNETTE. Ne vous inquiétez pas.

VÉRONIQUE. J'ai eu une très mauvaise réaction.

785 ANNETTE. Mais non... *(après un flottement gêné)*... Je me suis dit une chose dans la salle de bain...

VÉRONIQUE. Oui ?

ANNETTE. Nous sommes peut-être trop vite passés sur... Enfin je veux dire...

790 MICHEL. Dites, dites Annette.

ANNETTE. L'insulte aussi est une agression.

MICHEL. Bien sûr.

VÉRONIQUE. Ça dépend Michel.

MICHEL. Oui ça dépend.

795 ANNETTE. Ferdinand ne s'est jamais montré violent. Il ne peut pas l'avoir été sans raison.

ALAIN. Il s'est fait traiter de balance !... *(portable vibre)*... Pardon !... *(s'écarte avec des signes d'excuse exagérés à Annette)*... Oui... À condition qu'aucune victime ne s'exprime. Pas de vic-800 times. Je ne veux pas que vous soyez à côté de victimes !... On nie en bloc et s'il le faut on attaque le journal... On vous faxe le projet de communiqué Maurice *(raccroche)*... Si on me traite de balance, je m'énerve.

MICHEL. À moins que ce soit vrai.

805 ALAIN. Pardon ?

MICHEL. Je veux dire si c'est justifié.

ANNETTE. Mon fils est une balance ?

MICHEL. Mais non, je plaisantais.

ANNETTE. Le vôtre aussi si on va par là.

810 MICHEL. Comment ça le nôtre aussi ?

ANNETTE. Il a bien dénoncé Ferdinand.

MICHEL. Sur notre insistance !

VÉRONIQUE. Michel, on sort complètement du sujet.

ANNETTE. Peu importe. Sur votre insistance ou pas, il l'a 815 dénoncé.

ALAIN. Annette.

ANNETTE. Quoi Annette ? *(À Michel.)* Vous pensez que mon fils est une balance ?

MICHEL. Je ne pense rien du tout.

820 ANNETTE. Alors si vous ne pensez rien, ne dites rien. Ne faites pas ces réflexions insinuantes[1].

VÉRONIQUE. Annette, gardons notre calme. Michel et moi nous efforçons d'être conciliants[2], et modérés[3]…

ANNETTE. Pas si modérés.

825 VÉRONIQUE. Ah bon ? Pourquoi ?

ANNETTE. Modérés en surface.

ALAIN. Toutou, il faut vraiment que j'y aille…

ANNETTE. Sois lâche, vas-y.

ALAIN. Annette, en ce moment je risque mon plus gros client,

830 alors ces pinailleries[4] de parents responsables…

VÉRONIQUE. Mon fils a perdu deux dents. Deux incisives.

ALAIN. Oui, oui, on va finir par le savoir.

VÉRONIQUE. Dont une définitivement.

ALAIN. Il en aura d'autres, on va lui en mettre d'autres ! Des

835 mieux ! On lui a pas crevé le tympan !

ANNETTE. Nous avons tort de ne pas considérer l'origine du problème.

VÉRONIQUE. Il n'y a pas d'origine. Il y a un enfant de onze ans qui frappe. Avec un bâton.

---

1. Conduisant à l'idée que Ferdinand est une « balance ».
2. Accommodants, arrangeants.
3. Calmes, sans exigences extrêmes.
4. Disputes pour des petits riens.

840 ALAIN. Armé d'un bâton.

MICHEL. Nous avons retiré ce mot.

ALAIN. Vous l'avez retiré parce que nous avons émis une objection[1].

MICHEL. Nous l'avons retiré sans discuter.

845 ALAIN. Un mot qui exclut délibérément l'erreur, la maladresse, qui exclut l'enfance.

VÉRONIQUE. Je ne suis pas sûre de pouvoir supporter ce ton.

ALAIN. Nous avons du mal à nous accorder vous et moi, depuis le début.

850 VÉRONIQUE. Monsieur, il n'y a rien de plus odieux que de s'entendre reprocher ce qu'on a soi-même considéré comme une erreur. Le mot « armé » ne convenait pas, nous l'avons changé. Cependant, si on s'en tient à la stricte définition du mot, son usage n'est pas abusif[2].

855 ANNETTE. Ferdinand s'est fait insulter et il a réagi. Si on m'attaque, je me défends surtout si je suis seule face à une bande.

MICHEL. Ça vous a requinquée de dégobiller.

ANNETTE. Vous mesurez la grossièreté de cette phrase.

MICHEL. Nous sommes des gens de bonne volonté. Tous les 860 quatre, j'en suis sûr. Pourquoi se laisser déborder par des irritations, des crispations inutiles ?...

VÉRONIQUE. Oh Michel, ça suffit ! Cessons de vouloir temporiser. Puisque nous sommes modérés en surface, ne le soyons plus !

---

1. Un argument opposé.
2. Exagéré.

865 MICHEL. Non, non, je refuse de me laisser entraîner sur cette pente.

ALAIN. Quelle pente ?

MICHEL. La pente lamentable où ces deux petits cons nous ont mis ! Voilà !

870 ALAIN. J'ai peur que Véro n'adhère pas à cette vision des choses.

VÉRONIQUE. Véronique !

ALAIN. Pardon.

VÉRONIQUE. Bruno est un petit con maintenant le pauvre.
875 C'est un comble !

ALAIN. Bon, allez, là vraiment il faut que je vous quitte.

ANNETTE. Moi aussi.

VÉRONIQUE. Allez-y, allez-y, moi je lâche prise.

Le téléphone des Houllié sonne.

880 MICHEL. Allô ?... Ah maman... Non, non, nous sommes avec des amis mais dis-moi. ... Oui, supprime-les, fais ce qu'ils te disent. ... Tu prends de l'Antril ? ! Attends, attends maman ne quitte pas... *(À Alain.)* C'est l'Antril votre saloperie ? Ma mère en prend !...

885 ALAIN. Des milliers de gens en prennent.

MICHEL. Alors celui-là tu l'arrêtes immédiatement. Tu entends maman ? Sur-le-champ. ... Ne discute pas. Je t'expliquerai. ... Tu dis au docteur Perolo que c'est moi qui te l'interdis. ... Pourquoi rouges ?... Pour que qui te voie ?... C'est

890 complètement idiot… Bon, on en reparle tout à l'heure. Je t'embrasse maman. Je te rappelle *(il raccroche)*… Elle a loué des béquilles rouges pour ne pas se faire écraser par des camions. Au cas où dans son état elle irait se balader la nuit sur une autoroute. On lui donne de l'Antril pour son hypertension !

895 ALAIN. Si elle en prend et qu'elle a l'air normal, je la fais citer comme témoin. Je n'avais pas une écharpe ? Ah la voilà.

MICHEL. Je n'apprécie pas du tout votre cynisme[1]. Si ma mère présente le moindre symptôme, vous me verrez en tête d'une class action[2].

900 ALAIN. On l'aura de toute façon.

MICHEL. Je le souhaite.

ANNETTE. Au revoir madame…

VÉRONIQUE. Ça ne sert à rien de bien se comporter. L'honnêteté est une idiotie, qui ne fait que nous affaiblir et nous 905 désarmer…

ALAIN. Bon, allons-y Annette, on en a assez pour aujourd'hui en prêches et sermons[3].

MICHEL. Partez, partez. Mais laissez-moi vous dire : depuis que je vous ai rencontrés, il me semble que, comment s'appelle-910 t-il, Ferdinand a des circonstances assez atténuantes.

ANNETTE. Quand vous avez tué ce hamster…

MICHEL. Tué ? !

---

1. Fait d'ignorer les conventions, les règles et la morale.
2. Action de groupe.
3. Discours qui visent à convaincre les auditeurs de se conduire selon la bonne morale (vocabulaire religieux).

ANNETTE. Oui.

MICHEL. J'ai tué le hamster ?!

915 ANNETTE. Oui. Vous vous efforcez de nous culpabiliser, vous avez mis la vertu dans votre poche alors que vous êtes un assassin vous-même.

MICHEL. Je n'ai absolument pas tué ce hamster !

ANNETTE. C'est pire. Vous l'avez laissé tremblant d'angoisse 920 dans un milieu hostile[1]. Ce pauvre hamster a dû être mangé par un chien ou un rat.

VÉRONIQUE. Ça c'est vrai ! Ça c'est vrai !

MICHEL. Comment ça, ça c'est vrai !

VÉRONIQUE. Ça c'est vrai. Qu'est-ce que tu veux ! C'est 925 affreux ce qui a dû arriver à cette bête.

MICHEL. Je pensais que le hamster serait heureux en liberté, pour moi il allait se mettre à courir dans le caniveau ivre de joie !

VÉRONIQUE. Il ne l'a pas fait.

ANNETTE. Et vous l'avez abandonné.

930 MICHEL. Je ne peux pas toucher ces bêtes ! Je ne peux pas toucher cette famille-là, merde, tu le sais bien Véro !

VÉRONIQUE. Il a peur des rongeurs.

MICHEL. Oui, je suis effrayé par les rongeurs, les reptiles me terrorisent, je n'ai aucune affinité avec ce qui est près du sol ! 935 Voilà !

ALAIN *(à Véronique)*. Et vous, pourquoi vous n'êtes pas descendue le chercher ?

---

1. Dangereux, qui ne lui convenait pas.

VÉRONIQUE. Mais j'ignorais tout voyons ! Michel nous a dit aux enfants et à moi que le hamster s'était enfui le lendemain
940 matin. Je suis descendue tout de suite, tout de suite, j'ai fait le tour du pâté, je suis même allée à la cave.

MICHEL. Véronique, je trouve odieux d'être subitement sur la sellette[1] pour cette histoire de hamster que tu as cru bon de raconter. C'est une affaire personnelle qui ne regarde que nous
945 et qui n'a rien à voir avec la situation présente ! Et je trouve inconcevable[2] de me faire traiter d'assassin ! Dans ma maison !

VÉRONIQUE. Qu'est-ce que ta maison a à voir là-dedans ?

MICHEL. Une maison dont j'ouvre les portes, dont j'ouvre grand les portes dans un esprit de conciliation, à des gens qui
950 devraient m'en savoir gré[3] !

ALAIN. Vous continuez à vous jeter des fleurs, c'est merveilleux.

ANNETTE. Vous n'éprouvez pas de remords ?

MICHEL. Je n'éprouve aucun remords. Cet animal m'a tou-
955 jours répugné. Je suis ravi qu'il ne soit plus là.

VÉRONIQUE. Michel c'est ridicule.

MICHEL. Qu'est-ce qui est ridicule ? Tu deviens folle toi aussi ? Leur fils tabasse Bruno et on me fait chier pour un hamster ?

VÉRONIQUE. Tu t'es très mal comporté avec ce hamster, tu
960 ne peux pas le nier.

MICHEL. Je me fous de ce hamster !

---

1. Interrogé comme un accusé.
2. Impensable.
3. M'en être reconnaissant.

VÉRONIQUE. Tu ne pourras pas t'en foutre ce soir avec ta fille.

MICHEL. Qu'elle vienne celle-là ! Je ne vais pas me faire dicter ma conduite par une morveuse de neuf ans !

965 ALAIN. Là je le rejoins, à cent pour cent.

VÉRONIQUE. C'est lamentable.

MICHEL. Attention Véronique, attention, jusqu'à maintenant je me suis montré pondéré[1] mais je suis à deux doigts de verser de l'autre côté.

970 ANNETTE. Et Bruno ?

MICHEL. Quoi Bruno ?

ANNETTE. Il n'est pas triste.

MICHEL. Bruno a d'autres soucis à mon avis.

VÉRONIQUE. Bruno était moins attaché à Grignote.

975 MICHEL. Quel nom grotesque ça aussi !

ANNETTE. Si vous n'éprouvez aucun remords, pourquoi voulez-vous que notre fils en éprouve ?

MICHEL. Je vais vous dire, toutes ces délibérations[2] à la con, j'en ai par-dessus la tête. On a voulu être sympathiques, on a 980 acheté des tulipes, ma femme m'a déguisé en type de gauche, mais la vérité est que je n'ai aucun self-control, je suis un caractériel[3] pur.

ALAIN. On l'est tous.

VÉRONIQUE. Non. Non. Je regrette, nous ne sommes pas tous 985 des caractériels.

---

1. Mesuré dans ses réactions.
2. Dans un procès, discussions pour savoir si l'accusé est coupable.
3. Présentant des troubles du caractère, sujet à des sautes d'humeur pouvant être violentes.

ALAIN. Pas vous, bon.

VÉRONIQUE. Pas moi non, Dieu merci.

MICHEL. Pas toi darji, pas toi, toi tu es une femme évoluée, tu es à l'abri des dérapages.

990 VÉRONIQUE. Pourquoi tu m'agresses ?

MICHEL. Je ne t'agresse pas. Au contraire.

VÉRONIQUE. Si, tu m'agresses, tu le sais.

MICHEL. Tu as organisé ce petit raout[1], je me suis laissé embrigader[2]…

995 VÉRONIQUE. Tu t'es laissé embrigader ?…

MICHEL. Oui.

VÉRONIQUE. C'est odieux.

MICHEL. Pas du tout. Tu milites pour la civilisation, c'est tout à ton honneur.

1000 VÉRONIQUE. Je milite pour la civilisation, parfaitement ! Et heureusement qu'il y a des gens qui le font ! *(Au bord des larmes.)* Tu trouves que c'est mieux d'être un caractériel ?

ALAIN. Allons, allons…

VÉRONIQUE *(idem)*. C'est normal de reprocher à quelqu'un
1005 de ne pas être caractériel ?…

ANNETTE. Personne ne dit ça. Personne ne vous fait ce reproche.

VÉRONIQUE. Si !… *(elle pleure)*.

ALAIN. Mais non !

---

1. **Réunion mondaine.**
2. **Se laisser influencer pour rejoindre une personne ou un groupe qui réduit la liberté de pensée individuelle.**

1010 VÉRONIQUE. Qu'est-ce qu'il fallait faire ? Porter plainte ? Ne pas se parler et s'entretuer par assurances interposées ?

MICHEL. Arrête Véro...

VÉRONIQUE. Arrête quoi ? !...

MICHEL. C'est disproportionné...

1015 VÉRONIQUE. Je m'en fiche ! On s'efforce d'échapper à la mesquinerie[1]... et on finit humilié[2] et complètement seul...

ALAIN *(portable ayant vibré)*. ... Oui... « Qu'ils le prouvent ! »... « Prouvez-le »... Mais de mon point de vue, il vaudrait mieux ne pas répondre...

1020 MICHEL. On est tout le temps seul ! Partout ! Qui veut un petit coup de rhum ?

ALAIN. ... Maurice, je suis en rendez-vous, je vous rappelle du bureau... *(coupe)*.

VÉRONIQUE. Voilà. Je vis avec un être complètement négatif.

1025 ALAIN. Qui est négatif ?

MICHEL. Moi.

VÉRONIQUE. C'était la pire idée du monde ! On n'aurait jamais dû faire cette réunion !

MICHEL. Je te l'avais dit.

1030 VÉRONIQUE. Tu me l'avais dit ?

MICHEL. Oui.

VÉRONIQUE. Tu m'avais dit que tu voulais pas faire cette réunion ? !

MICHEL. Je ne trouvais pas que c'était une bonne idée.

---

1. Bassesse.
2. Blessé dans son amour-propre.

1035 ANNETTE. C'était une bonne idée…

MICHEL. Je vous en prie!… *(levant la bouteille de rhum).* Quelqu'un en veut?…

VÉRONIQUE. Tu m'avais dit que ce n'était pas une bonne idée, Michel?!

1040 MICHEL. Il me semble.

VÉRONIQUE. Il te semble!

ALAIN. Un fond de verre je veux bien.

ANNETTE. Tu ne dois pas y aller?

ALAIN. Je peux boire un petit verre, au point où on en est.

1045 *(Michel sert Alain.)*

VÉRONIQUE. Regarde-moi dans les yeux et répète que nous n'étions pas d'accord sur cette question!

ANNETTE. Calmez-vous, Véronique, calmez-vous, ça n'a pas de sens…

1050 VÉRONIQUE. Qui a empêché qu'on touche au clafoutis ce matin? Qui a dit, on garde le reste du clafoutis pour les Reille?! Qui l'a dit?!

ALAIN. C'était sympa ça.

MICHEL. Quel rapport?

1055 VÉRONIQUE. Comment quel rapport?!

MICHEL. Quand on reçoit des gens, on reçoit des gens.

VÉRONIQUE. Tu mens, tu mens! Il ment!

ALAIN. Vous savez, personnellement, ma femme a dû me traîner. Quand on est élevé dans une idée johnwaynienne de la

1060 virilité, on n'a pas envie de régler ce genre de situation à coups de conversations.

MICHEL. Ha, ha !

ANNETTE. Je croyais que c'était Ivanhoé, le modèle.

ALAIN. C'est la même lignée.

1065 MICHEL. C'est complémentaire.

VÉRONIQUE. Complémentaire ! Jusqu'où tu vas t'humilier Michel !

ANNETTE. Je l'ai traîné pour rien visiblement.

ALAIN. Tu espérais quoi toutou ? – C'est vrai que c'est ridi-
1070 cule ce surnom. – Une révélation de l'harmonie universelle[1] ? Extra ce rhum.

MICHEL. Ah ! N'est-ce pas ! Cœur de Chauffe, quinze ans d'âge, direct de Sainte-Rose.

VÉRONIQUE. Et les tulipes, c'est qui ! J'ai dit c'est dommage
1075 qu'on n'ait plus de tulipes mais je n'ai pas demandé qu'on se rue à Mouton-Duvernet dès l'aube.

ANNETTE. Ne vous mettez pas dans cet état Véronique, c'est idiot.

VÉRONIQUE. C'est lui les tulipes ! Lui seul ! On n'a pas le droit
1080 de boire nous deux ?

ANNETTE. Nous en voulons aussi Véronique et moi. Amusant entre parenthèses quelqu'un qui se réclame d'Ivanhoé et de John Wayne et qui n'est pas capable de tenir une souris dans sa main.

1085 MICHEL. STOP avec ce hamster ! Stop !… *(Il sert un verre de rhum à Annette.)*

---

1. Théorie selon laquelle chaque chose et chaque être a naturellement sa place dans l'univers.

VÉRONIQUE. Ha, ha ! C'est vrai, c'est risible !

ANNETTE. Et elle ?

MICHEL. Je ne pense pas que ce soit nécessaire.

1090 VÉRONIQUE. Sers-moi Michel.

MICHEL. Non.

VÉRONIQUE. Michel !

MICHEL. Non.

Véronique tente de lui arracher la bouteille des mains.
1095 *Michel résiste.*

ANNETTE. Qu'est-ce qui vous prend Michel ? !

MICHEL. Allez, tiens, vas-y ! Bois, bois, quelle importance.

ANNETTE. C'est mauvais pour vous l'alcool ?

VÉRONIQUE. C'est excellent. De toute façon qu'est-ce qui
1100 peut être mauvais ?… *(elle s'effondre).*

ALAIN. Bon… Alors, je ne sais pas…

VÉRONIQUE *(à Alain)*. … Monsieur, enfin…

ANNETTE. Alain.

VÉRONIQUE. Alain, nous n'avons pas d'atomes crochus vous
1105 et moi mais voyez, je vis avec un homme qui a décidé une bonne fois pour toutes que la vie était médiocre, c'est très difficile de vivre avec un homme qui s'est blotti dans ce parti pris, qui ne veut rien changer, qui ne s'emballe pour rien…

MICHEL. Il s'en tape. Il s'en tape complètement.

1110 VÉRONIQUE. On a besoin de croire… de croire à une correction possible, non ?

MICHEL. C'est la dernière personne à qui tu peux raconter tout ça.

VÉRONIQUE. Je parle à qui je veux, merde !

1115 MICHEL *(le téléphone sonne)*. Qui nous fait chier encore ?… Oui maman… Il va bien. Enfin il va bien, il est édenté mais il va bien… Si, il a mal. Il a mal mais ça passera. Maman je suis occupé là, je te rappelle.

ANNETTE. Il a encore mal ?

1120 VÉRONIQUE. Non.

ANNETTE. Pourquoi inquiéter votre mère ?

VÉRONIQUE. Il ne peut pas faire autrement. Il faut toujours qu'il l'inquiète.

MICHEL. Bon ça suffit maintenant Véronique ! C'est quoi ce 1125 psychodrame[1] ?

ALAIN. Véronique, est-ce qu'on s'intéresse à autre chose qu'à soi-même ? On voudrait bien tous croire à une correction possible. Dont on serait l'artisan et qui serait affranchie de notre propre bénéfice[2]. Est-ce que ça existe ? Certains hommes 1130 traînent, c'est leur manière, d'autres refusent de voir le temps passer, battent le fer, quelle différence ? Les hommes s'agitent jusqu'à ce qu'ils soient morts. L'éducation, les malheurs du monde… Vous écrivez un livre sur le Darfour, bon, je comprends qu'on puisse se dire, tiens, je vais prendre un massacre,

---

1. Conflit spectaculaire ou jeu théâtral improvisé dans le but de soigner les participants qui y expriment leurs problèmes.
2. Dont on ne retirerait aucune satisfaction personnelle autre que philosophique.

1135 il n'y a que ça dans l'histoire, et je vais écrire dessus. On se sauve comme on peut.

VÉRONIQUE. Je n'écris pas ce livre pour me sauver moi. Vous ne l'avez pas lu, vous ne savez pas ce qu'il y a dedans.

ALAIN. Peu importe.

1140 *Flottement.*

VÉRONIQUE. C'est terrible cette odeur de *Kouros*!…

MICHEL. Abominable.

ALAIN. Vous n'y avez pas été de main morte.

ANNETTE. Pardon.

1145 VÉRONIQUE. Vous n'y êtes pour rien. C'est moi qui ai pulvérisé névrotiquement[1]. … Et pourquoi ne peut-on être légers, pourquoi faut-il toujours que les choses soient exténuantes[2] ?…

ALAIN. Vous raisonnez trop. Les femmes raisonnent trop.

ANNETTE. Une réponse originale, qui vous déconcerte agréa-1150 blement je suppose.

VÉRONIQUE. Je ne sais pas ce que veut dire raisonner trop. Et je ne vois pas à quoi servirait l'existence sans une conception morale du monde[3].

MICHEL. Voyez ma vie !

1155 VÉRONIQUE. Tais-toi ! Tais-toi ! J'exècre cette connivence[4] minable ! Tu me dégoûtes !

---

1. De façon malade, dérangée.
2. Très fatigantes.
3. Idée selon laquelle le monde est régi par un ensemble de valeurs réparties entre le bien et le mal.
4. Je déteste cette complicité.

MICHEL. Un peu d'humour s'il te plaît.

VÉRONIQUE. Je n'ai aucun humour. Et je n'ai pas l'intention d'en avoir.

1160 MICHEL. Moi je dis, le couple, la plus terrible épreuve que Dieu puisse nous infliger.

ANNETTE. Parfait.

MICHEL. Le couple, et la vie de famille.

ANNETTE. Vous n'êtes pas censé nous faire partager vos vues

1165 Michel. Je trouve ça même un peu indécent[1].

VÉRONIQUE. Ça ne le gêne pas.

MICHEL. Vous n'êtes pas d'accord ?

ANNETTE. Ces considérations sont hors de propos. Alain, dis quelque chose.

1170 ALAIN. Il a le droit de penser ce qu'il veut.

ANNETTE. Il n'est pas obligé d'en faire la publicité.

ALAIN. Oui, bon, peut-être…

ANNETTE. On se fiche de leur vie conjugale. On est là pour régler un problème d'enfants, on se fiche de leur vie conjugale.

1175 ALAIN. Oui, enfin…

ANNETTE. Enfin quoi ? Qu'est-ce que tu veux dire ?

ALAIN. C'est lié.

MICHEL. C'est lié ! Bien sûr que c'est lié !

VÉRONIQUE. Que Bruno se fasse casser deux dents est lié à

1180 notre vie conjugale ? !

MICHEL. Évidemment.

---

1. Qui n'est pas convenable, impudique.

ANNETTE. Nous ne vous suivons pas.

MICHEL. Renversez la proposition. Et admirez la situation où nous sommes. Les enfants absorbent notre vie, et la désa-
1185 grègent[1]. Les enfants nous entraînent au désastre, c'est une loi. Quand tu vois les couples qui s'embarquent en riant dans le matrimonial[2], tu te dis ils ne savent pas, ils ne savent rien les pauvres, ils sont contents. On ne vous dit rien au départ. J'ai un copain de l'armée qui va avoir un enfant avec une nouvelle
1190 fille. Je lui ai dit, un enfant à nos âges, quelle folie ! Les dix, quinze ans qui nous restent de bons avant le cancer ou le stroke[3], tu vas te faire chier avec un môme ?

ANNETTE. Vous ne pensez pas ce que vous dites.

VÉRONIQUE. Il le pense.

1195 MICHEL. Bien sûr que je le pense. Je pense même pire.

VÉRONIQUE. Oui.

ANNETTE. Vous vous avilissez[4] Michel.

MICHEL. Ah bon ? Ha, ha !

ANNETTE. Arrêtez de pleurer Véronique, vous voyez bien que
1200 ça le galvanise[5].

MICHEL *(à Alain qui remplit son verre vide)*. Allez-y, allez-y, exceptionnel non ?

ALAIN. Exceptionnel.

---

1. Détruisent.
2. Mariage.
3. L'accident vasculaire cérébral.
4. Vous vous rendez mauvais, méprisable.
5. Rend plus fort.

MICHEL. Je peux vous offrir un cigare ?...

205 VÉRONIQUE. Non, pas de cigare ici !

ALAIN. Tant pis.

ANNETTE. Tu ne t'apprêtais pas à fumer un cigare Alain !

ALAIN. Je fais ce que je veux Annette, si je veux accepter un cigare, j'accepte un cigare. Que je ne fumerai pas pour ne pas 210 énerver Véronique qui est déjà plus qu'à cran. Elle a raison, arrêtez de renifler, quand une femme pleure, un homme est aussitôt poussé aux dernières extrémités[1]. Encore que le point de vue de Michel, j'ai le regret de le dire, soit parfaitement fondé *(vibration du portable)*... Oui Serge... Vas-y... Mets 215 Paris, le... et une heure précise...

ANNETTE. C'est infernal !

ALAIN *(s'écartant et à voix feutrée pour échapper au courroux[2])*... L'heure à laquelle tu l'envoies. Il faut que ce soit tout chaud sorti du four. ... Non, pas « s'étonne ». « Dénonce ». S'étonne c'est 220 mou...

ANNETTE. Je vis ça du matin au soir, du matin au soir il est accroché à ce portable ! Nous avons une vie hachée par le portable !

ALAIN. Heu... Une seconde... *(couvrant le téléphone)*... 225 Annette, c'est très important !...

ANNETTE. C'est toujours très important. Ce qui se passe à distance est toujours plus important.

---

1. À bout.
2. À la colère.

ALAIN *(reprenant)*. … Vas-y… Oui… Pas « procédé ». « Manœuvre ». Une manœuvre, qui intervient à quinze jours de
1230 la reddition des comptes etc.

ANNETTE. Dans la rue, à table, n'importe où…

ALAIN. … Une étude entre guillemets ! Tu mets étude entre guillemets…

ANNETTE. Je ne dis plus rien. Capitulation totale. J'ai de nou-
1235 veau envie de vomir.

MICHEL. Où est la cuvette ?

VÉRONIQUE. Je ne sais pas.

ALAIN. … Tu n'as qu'à me citer : « Il s'agit d'une lamentable tentative de manipulation du cours… »

1240 VÉRONIQUE. Elle est là. Je vous en prie, allez-y.

MICHEL. Véro.

VÉRONIQUE. Tout va bien. On est équipés maintenant.

ALAIN. « … du cours et de déstabilisation de mon client », affirme maître Reille, avocat de la société Verenz-Pharma…
1245 AFP, Reuter[1], presse généraliste, presse spécialisée, tutti frutti… *(raccroche)*.

MICHEL. Elle a de nouveau envie de vomir.

ALAIN. Mais qu'est-ce que tu as !

ANNETTE. Ta tendresse me touche.

1250 ALAIN. Je m'inquiète !

ANNETTE. Excuse-moi. Je n'avais pas compris.

ALAIN. Oh Annette, je t'en prie ! On ne va pas s'y mettre nous

1. Agences de presse.

aussi ! Ils s'engueulent, leur couple est déliquescent[1], on n'est pas obligés de leur faire concurrence !

1255 VÉRONIQUE. Qu'est-ce qui vous permet de dire que notre couple est déliquescent ! De quel droit ?

ALAIN *(portable vibre)*... On vient de me le lire. On vous l'envoie Maurice... Manipulation, manipulation du cours. À tout de suite *(raccroche)*... Ce n'est pas moi qui le dis c'est 1260 François.

VÉRONIQUE. Michel.

ALAIN. Michel, pardon.

VÉRONIQUE. Je vous défends de porter le moindre jugement sur notre famille.

1265 ALAIN. Ne portez pas de jugement sur mon fils non plus.

VÉRONIQUE. Mais ça n'a rien à voir ! Votre fils a brutalisé le nôtre !

ALAIN. Ils sont jeunes, ce sont des gamins, de tout temps les gamins se sont castagnés[2] dans les cours de récré. C'est une loi 1270 de la vie.

VÉRONIQUE. Non, non !...

ALAIN. Mais si. Il faut un certain apprentissage pour substituer le droit à la violence. À l'origine je vous rappelle, le droit c'est la force.

1275 VÉRONIQUE. Chez les hommes préhistoriques peut-être. Pas chez nous.

---

1. Pas solide, en train de s'effondrer.
2. Battus.

ALAIN. Chez nous ! Expliquez-moi chez nous.

VÉRONIQUE. Vous me fatiguez, je suis fatiguée de ces conversations.

1280 ALAIN. Véronique, moi je crois au dieu du carnage. C'est le seul qui gouverne, sans partage, depuis la nuit des temps. Vous vous intéressez à l'Afrique n'est-ce pas… *(à Annette qui a un haut-le-cœur)*… Ça ne va pas ?…

ANNETTE. Ne t'occupe pas de moi.

1285 ALAIN. Mais si.

ANNETTE. Tout va bien.

ALAIN. Il se trouve que je reviens du Congo, voyez-vous. Là-bas, des gosses sont entraînés à tuer à l'âge de huit ans. Dans leur vie d'enfant, ils peuvent tuer des centaines de gens, à la

1290 machette, au twelve[1], au kalachnikov[1], au grenade launcher[2], alors comprenez que lorsque mon fils casse une dent, même deux, à un camarade avec une tige de bambou, square de l'Aspirant-Dunant, je sois moins disposé que vous à l'effroi et à l'indignation.

1295 VÉRONIQUE. Vous avez tort.

ANNETTE *(accentuant l'accent anglais)*. Grenade launcher !…

ALAIN. Oui, c'est comme ça que ça s'appelle.

Annette crache dans la cuvette.

MICHEL. Ça va ?

---

1. Types d'armes à feu dont les noms sont donnés respectivement en anglais et en russe.
2. Mot anglais signifiant « lanceur ».

1300 ANNETTE. … Parfaitement.

ALAIN. Mais qu'est-ce que tu as ? Qu'est-ce qu'elle a ?

ANNETTE. C'est de la bile ! C'est rien !

VÉRONIQUE. Ne m'apprenez pas l'Afrique. Je suis très au fait du martyre africain, je suis plongée dedans depuis des mois…

1305 ALAIN. Je n'en doute pas. D'ailleurs le procureur de la CPI[1] a ouvert une enquête sur le Darfour…

VÉRONIQUE. Vous ne pensez pas me l'apprendre ?

MICHEL. Ne la lancez pas là-dessus ! Par pitié !

Véronique se jette sur son mari et le tape, plusieurs fois, avec un
1310 *désespoir désordonné et irrationnel.*
Alain la tire.

ALAIN. Je commence à vous trouver sympathique vous savez !

VÉRONIQUE. Pas moi !

MICHEL. Elle se déploie pour la paix et la stabilité dans le
1315 monde.

VÉRONIQUE. Tais-toi !

Annette a un haut-le-cœur.
Elle prend son verre de rhum et le porte à sa bouche.

MICHEL. Vous êtes sûre ?

1320 ANNETTE. Si, si, ça me fera du bien.

---

1. Cour pénale internationale.

Véronique l'imite.

VÉRONIQUE. Nous vivons en France. Nous ne vivons pas à Kinshasa[1] ! Nous vivons en France avec les codes de la société occidentale. Ce qui se passe square de l'Aspirant-Dunant relève
1325 des valeurs de la société occidentale ! À laquelle, ne vous déplaise, je suis heureuse d'appartenir !

MICHEL. Battre son mari doit faire partie des codes…

VÉRONIQUE. Michel, ça va mal se terminer.

ALAIN. Elle s'est jetée sur vous avec une furia[2]. À votre place,
1330 je serais attendri.

VÉRONIQUE. Je peux recommencer tout de suite.

ANNETTE. Il se moque de vous, vous vous en rendez compte ?

VÉRONIQUE. Je m'en fous.

ALAIN. Au contraire. La morale nous prescrit de dominer nos
1335 pulsions[3] mais parfois il est bon de ne pas les dominer. On n'a pas envie de baiser en chantant l'*Agnus Dei*[4]. On le trouve ici ce rhum ?

MICHEL. De ce millésime, m'étonnerait !

ANNETTE. Grenade launcher ! Ha, ha !…

1340 VÉRONIQUE *(idem)*. Grenade launcher, c'est vrai !

ALAIN. Oui. Grenade launcher.

---

1. Capitale de la République démocratique du Congo.
2. Grande ardeur.
3. Désirs incontrôlables d'origine biologique qui poussent les individus.
4. Dans les religions catholique et anglicane, acclamation récitée pendant la messe. Cette locution latine signifie « agneau de Dieu ».

ANNETTE. Pourquoi tu ne dis pas lanceur de grenades ?

ALAIN. Parce qu'on dit grenade launcher. Personne ne dit lanceur de grenades. De même qu'on ne dit pas canon de douze, 1345 on dit twelve.

ANNETTE. C'est qui « on » ?

ALAIN. Ça suffit Annette. Ça suffit.

ANNETTE. Les grands baroudeurs, comme mon mari, ont du mal, il faut les comprendre, à s'intéresser aux événements de 1350 quartier.

ALAIN. Exact.

VÉRONIQUE. Je ne vois pas pourquoi. Je ne vois pas pourquoi. Nous sommes citoyens du monde. Je ne vois pas pourquoi il faudrait lâcher sur le terrain de la proximité.

1355 MICHEL. Oh Véro ! Épargne-nous ces formules à la mords-moi le nœud !

VÉRONIQUE. Je vais le tuer.

ALAIN *(portable a vibré)*. ... Oui, oui enlève « lamentable »... « Grossière ». Il s'agit d'une grossière tentative de... Voilà...

1360 VÉRONIQUE. Elle a raison, ça devient intolérable !

ALAIN. ... Sinon il approuve le reste ?... Bon, bon. Très bien *(raccroche)*... Qu'est-ce qu'on disait ?... Grenade launcher ?...

VÉRONIQUE. Je disais, n'en déplaise à mon mari, qu'il n'y a pas d'endroit meilleur qu'un autre pour exercer notre vigilance.

365 ALAIN. Vigilance... Oui... Annette, c'est absurde de boire dans ton état...

ANNETTE. Quel état ? Au contraire.

ALAIN. C'est intéressant cette notion… *(portable)*… Oui, non, aucune interview avant la diffusion du communiqué…

1370 VÉRONIQUE. Monsieur, je vous somme d'interrompre cette conversation éprouvante !

ALAIN. … Surtout pas… Les actionnaires s'en foutront… Rappelle-lui la souveraineté des actionnaires…

Annette se dirige vers Alain, lui arrache le portable et… après
1375 *avoir brièvement cherché où le mettre… le plonge dans le vase de tulipes.*

ALAIN. Annette, qu'est-ce… !!!

ANNETTE. Et voilà.

VÉRONIQUE. Ha, ha ! Bravo !

1380 MICHEL *(horrifié)*. Oh là là !

ALAIN. Mais tu es complètement démente[1] ! Merde !!!

Il se rue vers le vase mais Michel qui l'a précédé sort l'appareil trempé.

MICHEL. Le séchoir ! Où est le séchoir ?! *(Il le trouve et le met*
1385 *aussitôt en marche direction le portable.)*

ALAIN. Il faut t'interner ma pauvre ! C'est ahurissant !… J'ai tout là-dedans !… Il est neuf, j'ai mis des heures à le configurer !

---

1. Folle.

MICHEL *(à Annette ; par-dessus le bruit infernal du séchoir).*
1390 Vraiment je ne vous comprends pas. C'est un geste irresponsable.

ALAIN. J'ai tout, j'ai ma vie entière…

ANNETTE. Sa vie entière !…

MICHEL *(toujours le bruit).* Attendez, on va peut-être le
1395 récupérer…

ALAIN. Mais non ! C'est foutu !…

MICHEL. On va retirer la batterie et la puce. Vous pouvez l'ouvrir ?

ALAIN *(essayant de l'ouvrir sans y croire).* J'y connais rien, je
1400 viens de l'avoir…

MICHEL. Montrez.

ALAIN. C'est foutu… Et ça les fait rire, ça les fait rire !…

MICHEL *(il l'ouvre sans difficulté).* Voilà. *(Réattaquant avec le séchoir après avoir disposé les éléments.)* Au moins toi Véronique,
1405 tu pourrais avoir le bon goût de ne pas trouver ça drôle !

VÉRONIQUE *(riant de bon cœur).* Mon mari aura passé son après-midi à sécher des choses !

ANNETTE. Ha, ha, ha !

Annette n'hésite pas à se resservir de rhum.
1410 *Michel, imperméable à tout humour, s'active avec le plus grand soin.*
Pendant un moment, seul le bruit du séchoir règne.
Alain est effondré.

ALAIN. Laissez mon vieux. Laissez. On ne peut rien faire…

1415 *Michel finit par arrêter le séchoir.*

MICHEL. Il faut attendre… *(après un flottement).* Vous voulez utiliser le téléphone ?…

Alain fait signe que non et qu'il s'en fout.

MICHEL. Je dois dire…

1420 ANNETTE. Qu'est-ce que vous voulez dire Michel ?

MICHEL. Non… Je ne vois même pas quoi dire.

ANNETTE. Moi je trouve qu'on se sent bien. On se sent mieux je trouve *(flottement)*… On se sent tranquilles, non ?… Les hommes sont tellement accrochés à leurs accessoires… Ça les 1425 diminue… Ça leur enlève toute autorité… Un homme doit être libre de ses mains… Je trouve. Même une mallette, ça me gêne. Un jour un homme m'a plu et puis je l'ai vu avec un sac rectangulaire en bandoulière, un sac en bandoulière d'homme, mais enfin c'était fini. Le sac en bandoulière c'est ce qu'il y a 1430 de pire. Mais le portable à portée de main est aussi ce qu'il y a de pire. Un homme doit donner l'impression d'être seul… Je trouve. Je veux dire de pouvoir être seul… Moi aussi j'ai une idée johnwaynienne de la virilité. Qu'est-ce qu'il avait lui ? Un colt. Un truc qui fait le vide… Un homme qui ne donne pas 1435 l'impression d'être un solitaire n'a pas de consistance… Alors Michel vous êtes content. Ça se désagrège un peu notre petit… Comment vous avez dit ?… J'ai oublié le mot… Mais finalement… on se sent presque bien… Je trouve.

MICHEL. Je vous préviens quand même que le rhum rend
1440 dingue.

ANNETTE. Je suis on ne peut plus normale.

MICHEL. Bien sûr.

ANNETTE. Je commence à voir les choses avec une agréable sérénité.

1445 VÉRONIQUE. Ha, ha! C'est la meilleure!... Une agréable sérénité!

MICHEL. Quant à toi darjeeling, je ne vois pas l'utilité de te déglinguer ouvertement.

VÉRONIQUE. Boucle-la.

1450 *Michel va chercher la boîte à cigares.*

MICHEL. Choisissez Alain. Détendez-vous.

VÉRONIQUE. On ne fume pas le cigare dans la maison!

MICHEL. Hoyo ou D4... Hoyo du maire, Hoyo du député...

VÉRONIQUE. On ne fume pas dans une maison où un enfant
1455 est asthmatique!

ANNETTE. Qui est asthmatique?

VÉRONIQUE. Notre fils.

MICHEL. On avait bien une saloperie de hamster.

ANNETTE. C'est vrai qu'un animal n'est pas recommandé
1460 quand on a de l'asthme.

MICHEL. Pas du tout recommandé!

ANNETTE. Même un poisson rouge peut s'avérer contre-indiqué.

VÉRONIQUE. Je suis obligée d'écouter ces inepties[1] ? *(Elle*
1465 *arrache des mains de Michel la cave à cigares qu'elle ferme brutalement.)* Je regrette, je suis sans doute la seule à ne pas voir les choses avec une agréable sérénité ! D'ailleurs, je n'ai jamais été aussi malheureuse. Je pense que c'est le jour de ma vie où j'aurai été la plus malheureuse.

1470 MICHEL. Boire te rend malheureuse.

VÉRONIQUE. Michel, chaque mot que tu prononces m'anéantit. Je ne bois pas. Je bois une goutte de ta merde de rhum que tu présentes comme si tu montrais le saint suaire[2] à des ouailles[3], je ne bois pas et je le regrette amèrement, je serais soulagée de
1475 pouvoir m'enfuir dans un petit verre au moindre chagrin.

ANNETTE. Mon mari aussi est malheureux. Regardez-le. Il est voûté. Il a l'air abandonné au bord d'un chemin. Je crois que c'est le jour le plus malheureux de sa vie aussi.

ALAIN. Oui.

1480 ANNETTE. Je suis désolée toutou.

Michel remet un coup de séchoir sur les éléments du portable.

VÉRONIQUE. Arrête ce séchoir ! Il est mort son truc.

MICHEL *(téléphone sonne)*. Oui !... Maman je t'ai dit que nous étions occupés... Parce que c'est un médicament qui peut te

---

1. Absurdités, sottises.
2. Pour les chrétiens, linge dans lequel fut enveloppé le corps de Jésus-Christ.
3. Chrétiens convaincus.

1485 tuer ! C'est du poison !... Quelqu'un va t'expliquer... *(passant le combiné à Alain)*... Dites-lui.

ALAIN. Dites-lui quoi ?...

MICHEL. Ce que vous savez sur votre cochonnerie.

ALAIN. ... Comment ça va madame ?...

1490 ANNETTE. Qu'est-ce qu'il peut lui dire ? Il ne sait rien !

ALAIN. ... Oui... Et vous avez mal ?... Bien sûr. Mais l'opération va vous sauver... L'autre jambe aussi, ah oui. Non, non, je ne suis pas orthopédiste... *(en aparté)*... Elle m'appelle docteur...

1495 ANNETTE. Docteur, c'est grotesque[1], raccroche !

ALAIN. Mais vous... je veux dire vous n'avez aucun problème d'équilibre ?... Mais non. Pas du tout. Pas du tout. N'écoutez pas ce qu'on vous dit. Néanmoins, c'est aussi bien si vous l'arrêtez pendant un moment. Le temps... le temps de vous faire

1500 opérer tranquillement... Oui, on sent que vous êtes en forme... *(Michel lui arrache le combiné.)*

MICHEL. Bon maman, tu as compris, tu arrêtes ce médicament, pourquoi faut-il que tu discutes tout le temps, tu l'arrêtes, tu fais ce qu'on te dit, je te rappelle... Je t'embrasse,

1505 on t'embrasse *(raccroche)*. Elle m'épuise. Qu'est-ce qu'on s'emmerde dans la vie !

ANNETTE. Bon alors, finalement ? Je reviens ce soir avec Ferdinand ? Faudrait se décider. On a l'air de s'en foutre. On est quand même là pour ça je vous signale.

---

1. **Ridicule.**

1510 VÉRONIQUE. Maintenant c'est moi qui vais avoir un malaise. Où est la cuvette ?

MICHEL *(retirant la bouteille de rhum de la portée d'Annette).* Ça suffit.

ANNETTE. À mon avis, il y a des torts des deux côtés. Voilà. 1515 Des torts des deux côtés.

VÉRONIQUE. Vous êtes sérieuse ?

ANNETTE. Pardon ?

VÉRONIQUE. Vous pensez ce que vous dites ?

ANNETTE. Je le pense. Oui.

1520 VÉRONIQUE. Notre fils Bruno, à qui j'ai dû donner deux Efferalgan codéinés[1] cette nuit a tort ?!

ANNETTE. Il n'est pas forcément innocent.

VÉRONIQUE. Foutez le camp ! Je vous ai assez vus *(elle se saisit du sac d'Annette et le balance vers la porte).* Foutez le camp !

1525 ANNETTE. Mon sac !… *(comme une petite fille).* Alain !…

MICHEL. Mais qu'est-ce qui se passe ? Elles sont déchaînées.

ANNETTE *(ramassant ce qui peut être éparpillé).* Alain, au secours !…

VÉRONIQUE. Alain-au-secours !

1530 ANNETTE. La ferme !… Elle a cassé mon poudrier ! Et mon vaporisateur ! *(à Alain).* Défends-moi, pourquoi tu ne me défends pas ?…

ALAIN. On s'en va *(il s'apprête à récupérer les éléments de son portable).*

---

1. Antidouleurs contenant un opiacé, c'est-à-dire un dérivé de l'opium.

1535 VÉRONIQUE. Je ne suis pas en train de l'étrangler !

ANNETTE. Qu'est-ce que je vous ai fait ?!

VÉRONIQUE. Il n'y a pas de torts des deux côtés ! On ne confond pas les victimes et les bourreaux !

ANNETTE. Les bourreaux !

1540 MICHEL. Oh tu fais chier Véronique, on en a marre de ce boniment simpliste[1] !

VÉRONIQUE. Que je revendique.

MICHEL. Oui, oui, tu revendiques, tu revendiques, ça déteint sur tout maintenant ton engouement pour les nègres du

1545 Soudan.

VÉRONIQUE. Je suis épouvantée. Pourquoi tu te montres sous ce jour horrible ?

MICHEL. Parce que j'ai envie. J'ai envie de me montrer sous un jour horrible.

1550 VÉRONIQUE. Un jour vous comprendrez l'extrême gravité de ce qui se passe dans cette partie du monde et vous aurez honte de votre inertie[2] et de ce nihilisme[3] infect.

MICHEL. Mais tu es formidable darjeeling, la meilleure d'entre nous !

1555 VÉRONIQUE. Oui. Oui.

ANNETTE. Filons Alain, ce sont des monstres ces gens ! *(Elle finit son verre et va reprendre la bouteille.)*

---

1. Discours trompeur qui simplifie la réalité.
2. Manque d'engagement.
3. Fait de ne croire en rien, en aucune valeur morale.

ALAIN *(l'en empêchant)*. … Arrête Annette.

ANNETTE. Non, je veux encore boire, je veux me saouler la
1560 gueule, cette conne balance mes affaires et personne ne bronche, je veux être ivre !

ALAIN. Tu l'es assez.

ANNETTE. Pourquoi tu laisses traiter ton fils de bourreau ? On vient dans leur maison pour arranger les choses et on se fait
1565 insulter, et brutaliser, et imposer des cours de citoyenneté planétaire, notre fils a bien fait de cogner le vôtre, et vos droits de l'homme je me torche avec !

MICHEL. Un petit coup de gnôle et hop le vrai visage apparaît. Où est passée la femme avenante et réservée, avec une dou-
1570 ceur de traits…

VÉRONIQUE. Je te l'avais dit ! Je te l'avais dit !

ALAIN. Qu'est-ce que vous aviez dit ?

VÉRONIQUE. Qu'elle était fausse. Elle est fausse cette femme. Je regrette.

1575 ANNETTE *(avec détresse)*. Ha, ha, ha !…

ALAIN. À quel moment vous l'avez dit ?

VÉRONIQUE. Quand vous étiez dans la salle de bains.

ALAIN. Vous la connaissiez depuis un quart d'heure mais vous saviez qu'elle était fausse.

1580 VÉRONIQUE. Je sens ça tout de suite chez les gens.

MICHEL. C'est vrai.

VÉRONIQUE. J'ai un feeling pour ce genre de choses.

ALAIN. Fausse, c'est-à-dire ?

ANNETTE. Je ne veux pas entendre ! Pourquoi tu m'obliges
1585 à supporter ça Alain !

ALAIN. Calme-toi toutou.

VÉRONIQUE. C'est une arrondisseuse d'angles. Point. En dépit de ses manières. Elle n'est pas plus concernée que vous.

MICHEL. C'est vrai.

1590 ALAIN. C'est vrai.

VÉRONIQUE. C'est vrai ! Vous dites c'est vrai ?

MICHEL. Ils s'en tapent ! Ils s'en tapent depuis le début, c'est évident ! Elle aussi, tu as raison !

ALAIN. Pas vous peut-être ? *(à Annette).* Laisse parler mon
1595 amour. Expliquez-moi en quoi vous êtes concerné Michel. Que veut dire ce mot d'abord ? Vous êtes plus crédible quand vous vous montrez sous un jour horrible. À vrai dire personne n'est concerné ici, sauf Véronique à qui il faut, c'est vrai, reconnaître cette intégrité[1].

1600 VÉRONIQUE. Ne me reconnaissez rien ! Ne me reconnaissez rien !

ANNETTE. Mais moi je le suis. Je suis tout à fait concernée.

ALAIN. Nous le sommes sous le mode hystérique[2] Annette, non comme des héros de la vie sociale. *(À Véronique.)* J'ai vu
1605 votre amie Jane Fonda l'autre jour à la télé, j'étais à deux doigts d'acheter un poster du Ku Klux Klan…

---

1. Honnêteté.
2. Avec des réactions excessives.

VÉRONIQUE. Pourquoi mon amie ? Qu'est-ce que Jane Fonda vient faire là-dedans !…

ALAIN. Parce que vous êtes de la même espèce. Vous faites
1610 partie de la même catégorie de femmes, les femmes investies, solutionnantes, ce n'est pas ce qu'on aime chez les femmes, ce qu'on aime chez les femmes c'est la sensualité, la folie, les hormones, les femmes qui font état de leur clairvoyance, les gardiennes du monde nous rebutent, même lui ce pauvre Michel,
1615 votre mari, est rebuté…

MICHEL. Ne parlez pas en mon nom !

VÉRONIQUE. On se fout complètement de ce que vous aimez chez les femmes ! D'où sort cette tirade ? Vous êtes un homme dont on se fout royalement de l'avis !

1620 ALAIN. Elle hurle. Quartier-maître sur un thonier au dix-neuvième siècle[1] !

VÉRONIQUE. Et elle, elle ne hurle pas ? ! Quand elle dit que son petit connard a bien fait de cogner le nôtre ?

ANNETTE. Il a bien fait, oui ! Au moins on n'a pas un petit
1625 pédé qui s'écrase !

VÉRONIQUE. Vous avez une balance, c'est mieux ?

ANNETTE. Partons Alain ! Qu'est-ce qu'on fait encore dans cette baraque ? *(Elle fait mine de partir puis revient vers les tulipes qu'elle gifle violemment. Les fleurs volent, se désagrègent et s'étalent*
1630 *partout.)* Et tiens, tiens, voilà ce que j'en fais de vos fleurs

---

1. S'exprimant comme un marin-pêcheur d'autrefois sur son bateau.

minables, vos tulipes hideuses !... Ha, ha, ha !... *(elle s'effondre en pleurs)*... C'est le pire jour de ma vie aussi.

Silence.
Un long temps de stupeur.
1635 *Michel ramasse quelque chose par terre.*

MICHEL *(à Annette)*. C'est à vous ?...
ANNETTE *(elle prend l'étui, l'ouvre et sort les lunettes)*. Merci...
MICHEL. Elles sont intactes ?...
ANNETTE. Oui...

1640 *Flottement.*

MICHEL. Moi je dis...

Alain entreprend de ramasser les tiges et les pétales.

MICHEL. Laissez.
ALAIN. Mais non...

1645 *Le téléphone sonne.*
Après une hésitation Véronique décroche.

VÉRONIQUE. Oui ma chérie... Ah bon... Mais tu pourras faire tes devoirs chez Annabelle ?... Non, non chérie on ne l'a

pas retrouvée… Oui, je suis allée jusqu'à Franprix. Mais tu sais,
1650 Grignote est très débrouillarde mon amour, je crois qu'il faut avoir confiance en elle. Tu penses qu'elle se plaisait dans une cage ?… Papa est triste, il ne voulait pas te faire de peine… Mais si. Mais si tu vas lui parler. Écoute mon amour, on est déjà assez embêtés avec ton frère… Elle mangera… elle mangera des
1655 feuilles… des glands, des marrons d'Inde… elle trouvera, elle sait ce qu'elle doit manger… des vers, des escargots, ce qui sera tombé des poubelles, elle est omnivore comme nous… À tout à l'heure mon trésor.

Flottement.

1660 MICHEL. Si ça se trouve, cette bête festoie à l'heure qu'il est.

VÉRONIQUE. Non.

Silence.

MICHEL. Qu'est-ce qu'on sait ?

Après-texte

POUR COMPRENDRE

GROUPEMENT DE TEXTES

INTERVIEW EXCLUSIVE

INFORMATION/DOCUMENTATION

APRÈS LA PREMIÈRE LECTURE

Lire

1 À la lumière de votre lecture, expliquez le titre de la pièce.

2 Page 9 : observez les didascalies. Quelles sont les formes de phrases utilisées ? Pourquoi ?

3 Le théâtre classique prône la règle des trois unités (*cf.* « À savoir » p. 83) : unités de lieu, de temps et d'action. Qu'en est-il dans cette pièce ?

4 Quelle didascalie récurrente trouve-t-on pages 11, 19, 20, 24 et 30 ?

5 Les pièces du théâtre classique comme celles de Molière sont divisées en actes et en scènes. Est-ce le cas pour *Le Dieu du carnage* ? Quel rôle joue la didascalie récurrente vue dans la question 4 ?

6 Quel différend a opposé les deux enfants ?

7 Quel problème tente de résoudre Alain par téléphone ?

8 Il y a dans la pièce plusieurs problèmes de communication : concernant les enfants, on apprend que Bruno ne voulait pas « dénoncer Ferdinand » (p. 12, l. 65) et « refusait de parler » (l. 69). De même, Alain, l'un des adultes, refuse de donner des informations à la presse. De quelles informations s'agit-il ? Les problèmes des adultes et des enfants sont-ils très différents ? Que pensez-vous de leurs conséquences ?

9 En vous aidant de la liste page 8, classez les prénoms des personnages dans l'ordre alphabétique. Quels sont les personnages les plus « primaires », c'est-à-dire situés au début de la liste, et quel est le personnage le plus culturellement évolué ?

10 Quels personnages jouent un rôle dans l'intrigue sans jamais apparaître sur scène ? Notez leur nom et leur lien avec les personnages présents.

11 Sur quel type de phrase se clôt la pièce ? Quel genre de fin est-ce donc ?

12 « Chassez le naturel, il revient au galop » : en quoi la pièce illustre-t-elle ce proverbe ?

Écrire

13 Présentez les deux couples en faisant le portrait de chacun des personnages (nom, métier, prénom de l'enfant, etc.).

14 Racontez la fable du hamster, c'est-à-dire le récit des actions accomplies par Michel concernant l'animal.

Chercher

15 Quelle est l'étymologie du terme « carnage » ? Donnez d'autres mots de la même famille.

16 Cherchez la définition de « huis clos », son origine étymologique, et des expressions dans lesquelles on rencontre ce terme.

17 Au CDI, consultez des pièces de théâtre appartenant à différentes époques. Comparez les didascalies initiales avec celles du texte de Yasmina Reza.

18 Cherchez le sens du mot « salon » aux XVIIe et XVIIIe siècles. Qui tenait salon à cette époque ? Qu'en est-il de nos jours ?

19 Cherchez dans un dictionnaire la définition des mots « culture » et « morale ».

À SAVOIR

VERS LE THÉÂTRE MODERNE

Au XVIIe siècle, deux genres dominent au théâtre : la comédie, avec Molière, et la tragédie, avec Corneille et Racine. La comédie a pour vocation de faire rire les spectateurs en montrant les personnages et la société sous leurs aspects ridicules. La tragédie doit émouvoir le public en mettant en scène des personnages exceptionnels en proie à une destinée fatale.

Au XVIIIe siècle, si la comédie triomphe, le drame bourgeois repousse peu à peu les limites entre les deux genres, offrant une critique de la société et une liberté de forme de plus en plus grande.

La comédie de mœurs, ou comédie légère, continue à séduire les spectateurs au XIXe siècle dans les vaudevilles de Labiche et Feydeau. On assiste, dans les théâtres des boulevards parisiens, à des pièces mettant en scène des maris et des femmes trompés, ou des naïfs dupés par de plus rusés. Les auteurs de la seconde moitié du XXe siècle, comme Jean Anouilh, Yasmina Reza ou Edward Albee (voir le groupement de textes en fin d'ouvrage), s'en inspirent et s'en détachent à la fois pour créer leurs œuvres. Elles restent fondées sur le quotidien, mais prennent une dimension plus profonde et plus intime. Dans *Le Dieu du carnage*, le conflit se déroule dans l'univers familier du salon de l'un des couples. L'originalité de la pièce réside dans le fait que l'auteur réussit à orienter une intrigue domestique (la dispute des deux garçons et son retentissement sur leurs parents) vers une problématique universelle reposant sur le conflit intérieur que nous connaissons tous entre notre naturel, parfois brutal, et les bonnes manières que nous ont inculquées des siècles d'éducation.

Lire

1 Quel niveau de langue utilise Véronique pour rédiger sa déclaration d'assurance (p. 9, l. 7-13) ?

2 Quelle relation existe-t-il entre les mots « armé » (l. 15), « muni » et « doté » (l. 16) ?

3 Quelle figure de style emploie Véronique page 12 lorsqu'elle désigne son fils par l'expression « cet enfant qui n'avait plus de visage, plus de dents » (l. 69) ? Quel est l'effet produit ?

4 Que sous-entend Michel lorsqu'il dit qu'il n'y avait pas « que de la bravoure » (l. 73) dans le comportement de son fils ?

5 Lignes 74 à 77 : en quoi les répliques de Véronique et d'Annette sont-elles comiques ?

6 Lignes 80 à 84 : quel style de discours (direct ou indirect) Michel et Véronique emploient-ils ? Quelle erreur syntaxique le texte reproduit-il ? Pourquoi ? Comparez cet extrait avec la réplique d'Alain (l. 86-98).

7 Véronique est écrivain et travaille à mi-temps dans « une librairie d'art et d'histoire » (l. 103). Quelles informations ce métier fournit-il sur le personnage ?

8 Pages 9 à 14 : quels sujets de conversation sont abordés (l. 1 à 133) ? Notez-les dans l'ordre chronologique.

9 Ligne 110 : quel type de phrase utilise Annette ? Comment la réplique suivante, prononcée par Véronique, indique qu'Annette aurait dû en utiliser un autre ? Lequel ?

10 Selon Michel, les hamsters ne sont « ni des animaux domestiques, ni des animaux sauvages » (l. 123) et on ne sait pas « où est leur milieu naturel » (l. 124). Qu'en pensez-vous ?

11 Au théâtre, la scène d'exposition présente les personnages et met l'intrigue en place. En quoi peut-on dire que les pages 9 à 14 (l. 1-133) constituent une scène d'exposition ? Quelles informations y apprend-on ?

Écrire

12 À l'aide des indications données page 12, de la ligne 65 à 84, écrivez une scène dans laquelle Véronique et Michel font avouer à Bruno, défiguré, le nom de celui qui l'a frappé. Vous intégrerez les didascalies nécessaires.

Chercher

13 En quoi consiste le métier d'une conseillère en gestion de patrimoine ?

14 Où se trouvent l'Éthiopie et l'Érythrée ?

15 Cherchez les antonymes des termes « muni » et « armé ».

Oral

16 Jouez le début de la scène (l. 7-31).

À SAVOIR

LES CONVENTIONS THÉÂTRALES

Le théâtre est un genre codé par un ensemble de règles, les conventions, qui sont liées aux contraintes de la représentation. Les textes sont en effet écrits pour être joués par des acteurs, dans un espace clos qu'il faut meubler d'un décor, afin d'être vus par un public.

Au XVIIe siècle, comédies et tragédies, découpées en actes et en scènes, étaient soumises à des règles rigoureuses, héritées du théâtre antique et des principes d'Aristote. D'abord, la règle des trois unités ordonnait à la pièce de se dérouler en un lieu unique (unité de lieu), en un seul jour (unité de temps), et selon une seule intrigue (unité d'action). De plus, les pièces obéissaient à la règle de bienséance. Les événements sanglants ou désagréables, susceptibles de choquer le spectateur, devaient se produire hors scène. Enfin, elles étaient régies par la règle de vraisemblance, de ressemblance avec la réalité. Ces règles sont maintenant caduques et les auteurs modernes sont libres d'écrire les pièces comme ils l'entendent.

Le rôle du metteur en scène est aujourd'hui déterminant. En effet, il doit proposer une interprétation cohérente du texte. Il crée l'espace scénique en imaginant les décors, les objets et l'éclairage, en se fondant sur les informations données par les dialogues et les didascalies. Il choisit également les acteurs qui vont incarner les personnages.

Yasmina Reza a elle-même mis en scène *Le Dieu du carnage* en France. Dans cette pièce qui se déroule à huis clos, le décor ne change pas, et il n'y pas de divisions en actes ni en scènes. Seules les entrées et les sorties de certains personnages, ainsi que les silences ordonnés par les didascalies sous la forme de « flottements », scandent le texte. La pièce a, de plus, l'originalité de faire intervenir sur scène des personnages qui ne s'y trouvent pas, offrant des dialogues à une seule voix par l'intermédiaire d'un moyen de communication moderne, le téléphone, qui propose un nouveau regard sur la construction du dialogue et du monologue.

Lire

1 Relisez le texte lignes 134 à 143. Quelle différence y a-t-il entre « se parler » et « s'excuser » ?

2 En vous aidant de la note du bas de la page 15, expliquez les propos de Michel : « on est un tas de terre glaise et de ça il faut faire quelque chose. Peut-être que ça ne prendra forme qu'à la fin. » (l. 152-153) De quelle « fin » parle-t-il ? Que pouvez-vous dire de l'emploi des pronoms « on » et « ça » ? Son propos a-t-il un rapport direct avec la conversation ?

3 Que dénote la réflexion d'Alain « au moins ça nous permet de découvrir une recette » (l. 200-201) sur ce qu'il pense du rendez-vous ?

4 Relisez l'ensemble des conversations téléphoniques d'Alain (p. 17-18, l. 206-228). Quel rôle jouent les points de suspension dans le texte ? Et dans la mise en scène ? En quoi la seconde tirade (l. 216-228) répond aux interrogations que le spectateur se pose à l'issue de la première ?

5 Lignes 213 à 214 : que nous indique la didascalie sur le comportement d'Alain ?

6 Un monologue est un discours fait sur scène par un personnage seul. Lignes 206 à 228, Alain parle-t-il aux personnages sur scène ? S'agit-il pour autant d'un monologue ?

7 À l'aide de l'encadré « À savoir » de l'étape 2, dites en quoi l'utilisation sur scène du téléphone change les conventions traditionnelles du théâtre.

8 Quel sujet de conversation provoque le « flottement souriant » indiqué par la didascalie page 19, ligne 250 ? Est-ce un sujet d'ordinaire comique ?

9 Page 20, ligne 265 : la didascalie indique un nouveau « flottement ». A-t-il la même valeur que le précédent (l. 250) ? En vous aidant de l'encadré « À savoir », définissez les registres employés dans chacun de ces deux passages.

10 Lignes 266 à 285 et lignes 357 à 362 : quels sont les personnages qui entrent ouvertement en conflit ? À quel sujet exactement ? Qui prend la mouche le premier ? Pour quelles raisons ?

11 Quel type de phrase emploie Véronique à plusieurs reprises (l. 266-297) ? Quel rôle joue-t-elle dans ce dialogue à quatre voix ?

12 Lignes 358 à 359 : quel mode verbal utilise Alain dans sa réplique ? Quelle valeur exprime-t-il ?

13 Les deux couples éduquent-ils leurs fils de la même façon ?

14 Observez les répliques d'Alain lignes 234 et 310 à 312. Que pensez-vous de la construction syntaxique de ces phrases ? Quels effets cela crée-t-il ?

Écrire

Argumentation

15 Relisez le texte des lignes 294 à 306 (p. 21-22). Pensez-vous qu'obliger les enfants à discuter est une solution valable pour résoudre le conflit qui les oppose ?

16 Annette et Alain amènent finalement Ferdinand chez les Houllié. Dans la voiture, Annette tente de le convaincre de l'importance de cette discussion pour sa réconciliation avec Bruno. Alain pense le contraire. Ferdinand donne également son avis. Écrivez cette scène, sans oublier d'indiquer par des didascalies le dispositif envisagé pour matérialiser le décor et le comportement des trois personnages.

Chercher

17 Documentez-vous sur la Cour pénale internationale. Depuis quand existe-t-elle ? Quel est son rôle ? Quels sont les États concernés ?

18 Documentez-vous sur le métier d'avocat.

Oral

19 Jouez la scène (l. 286-312).

20 Faites une lecture expressive de l'une des conversations téléphoniques d'Alain (l. 206-214 ou l. 216-228).

À SAVOIR

LE DRAME ET LE MÉLANGE DES REGISTRES

À l'époque du théâtre classique (XVIIe siècle), la tragédie devait susciter l'effroi, et la comédie le rire. Chaque genre dramatique avait donc son registre propre, sa tonalité. Le drame, qu'il soit bourgeois (XVIIIe siècle), romantique (XIXe siècle) ou moderne, met à bas cette distinction. Une pièce de théâtre peut provoquer un éventail de sentiments et jouer par conséquent sur plusieurs registres, tout en étant dominée par une tonalité générale. Ainsi, *Le Dieu du carnage* est une comédie dans laquelle les moments comiques (par exemple, l. 196-205) alternent avec des passages plus graves (l. 266-279), ou pathétiques, en suscitant la tristesse et la compassion du spectateur (l. 127-131), et même polémiques, en invitant à un débat d'idées avec plus ou moins d'agressivité (l. 356-362).

BRUNO, CHEF DE BANDE

PAGES 24 À 33

Lire

1 Quel couple révèle à l'autre le motif de la dispute des garçons ? Est-ce surprenant ?

2 Les générations des pères et des fils se ressemblent-elles ?

3 Page 28, ligne 451 : expliquez la réplique de Véronique. Quel mode verbal utilise-t-elle ?

4 Pages 29-30, lignes 492-528 : que pouvez-vous dire de la situation de communication ?

5 D'après vous, que veut dire Michel lorsqu'il compare son « métier ordinaire » (l. 538) au « drôle de métier » d'Alain (l. 533) ?

6 Qui dirige la conversation sur le métier de Michel (l. 532-560) ? Quelle est la réaction des femmes ? Lisez les répliques d'Alain à partir de la ligne 550 : que montrent-elles ? À quel genre de comique appartient cette scène, culminant avec la réplique de Michel (l. 552, p. 32) ?

Écrire

7 Véronique se trouve seule sur scène, après le départ des Reille. Dans un monologue, elle explique pourquoi elle pense qu'il est de son devoir de mère d'intervenir dans la dispute des enfants. Vous insérerez dans votre texte les didascalies nécessaires.

8 Récrivez le texte page 26 de la ligne 408 à 427, en ajoutant des répliques que les personnages prononceront *en aparté*, c'est-à-dire des répliques que, par convention, les autres personnages n'entendent pas.

Chercher

9 Documentez-vous sur la vie et les tableaux de Francis Bacon.

10 Cherchez quelles sont les valeurs de l'idéal chevaleresque.

11 Lisez *Monsieur de Pourceaugnac* de Molière ou visionnez une captation de la pièce.

À SAVOIR

LA DOUBLE ÉNONCIATION AU THÉÂTRE

On parle de double énonciation au théâtre, car les paroles des personnages ont un double destinataire : les autres personnages et le public. La double énonciation est présente à tous les niveaux du texte, de façon explicite ou implicite. Ainsi, quand les Reille et les Houllié font allusion à Monsieur de Pourceaugnac, Ivanhoé ou Spiderman, ils entrent en connivence avec le public, qui connaît lui aussi ces héros.

LE MALAISE D'ANNETTE

PAGES 33 À 41

Lire

1 Quel niveau de langue utilisent Alain pour parler à son collaborateur (l. 595 à 597) et Annette (dans les répliques suivantes) ? Quel est leur état d'esprit ?

2 Lignes 598 à 628 : à quoi assiste-t-on ?

3 Quelle convention du théâtre classique (XVIIe siècle) est bafouée dans cette scène (*cf.* « À savoir », p. 83) ?

4 Le malaise d'Annette crée du mouvement sur scène. Repérez les entrées et les sorties des personnages de la page 36 à 41 (l. 655-771).

5 En quoi la réplique de Michel (l. 660-661) fait-elle écho à une autre de ses répliques (l. 151-154, p. 15) ?

6 Pages 36-40 : quel sentiment Véronique nourrit-elle à l'égard de ses livres ?

7 En quoi peut-on dire que Michel est un homme d'action (p. 37-40) ?

8 Seuls, Véronique et Michel reviennent sur ce qui s'est passé (l. 706-736). Quel portrait font-ils de l'autre couple ?

Écrire

9 Seuls dans la salle de bains, Annette et Alain font le portrait de l'autre couple. Imaginez leur dialogue.

Chercher

10 Trouvez des informations sur la vie et la peinture d'Oskar Kokoschka et de Tsuguharu Foujita.

Oral

11 Lisez à plusieurs voix les portraits exécutés par Célimène dans *Le Misanthrope* de Molière (acte II, scène 4).

À SAVOIR

LES FONCTIONS DU THÉÂTRE

Tout d'abord, une pièce de théâtre divertit le spectateur. Mais elle peut aussi délivrer un message politique ou moralisateur : on parle alors de théâtre engagé. Elle contribue en outre à la purgation des passions, la catharsis, selon le terme d'Aristote : le spectateur éprouve de la compassion pour les personnages et en ressent une libération profitable. Enfin, les pièces nous font réfléchir à nos problèmes personnels et à ceux de la société. Dans *Le Dieu du carnage*, on s'interroge sur l'efficacité de l'engagement pour une grande cause (à l'image de Véronique pour l'Afrique) ou sur les limites de la connaissance que l'on a de l'autre, qu'il soit dans notre salon ou au Darfour.

Lire

1 Pages 42-45 : quel personnage mène le dialogue (l. 785-878) ? Est-ce surprenant ?

2 Lignes 797-803 : comment Alain fait-il le lien entre les effets secondaires de l'Antril et la bagarre de son fils ? Lignes 840 à 846 (p. 44) : relevez le vocabulaire qui montre qu'il confond son métier et son rôle de père.

3 La polémique reprise par Alain (l. 840) a débuté dès la première page. Que signifie le mot « délibérément » (l. 845) ? De quel mot déjà utilisé au début de la page 29 peut-on le rapprocher ?

4 Pourquoi les précautions que prend la mère de Michel avec ses béquilles (l. 886-894, p. 45-46) semblent-elles dérisoires ?

5 Lignes 903 à 905 : à qui s'adresse la réplique de Véronique ? Que pensez-vous de l'utilisation du dernier terme ?

6 Qu'est-ce que la « vertu » dont parle Annette (l. 916, p. 47) ? Quel est l'antonyme de ce mot ?

7 Quelle figure de style emploie Annette en traitant Michel d'assassin (l. 916) ? Quel est l'effet produit ? Cherchez une autre occurrence de cette figure de style dans les répliques de Michel page 47.

8 Annette demande à Michel s'il n'éprouve pas de « remords », c'est-à-dire un malaise dû à la sensation d'avoir mal agi (l. 953, p. 48). À quel domaine appartient ce terme ?

9 Montrez que Michel se révèle sous un nouveau jour (l. 978-1014, p. 49-51).

10 La question d'Annette (l. 976-977) fait écho à une réflexion de Michel (l. 631, p. 35). Relisez ces deux passages et comparez-les. Que montrent-ils à propos de l'éducation des enfants ?

11 Selon Michel, Véronique est « une femme évoluée » (l. 988). Elle rajoute elle-même qu'elle « milite pour la civilisation » (l. 1000). Qu'entendent-ils par ces expressions ?

12 Page 51 : que montre la réplique d'Alain (l. 1022-1023) à propos de ce qui se joue pour lui dans le salon et au téléphone ? Lequel des deux sujets devient le plus important ? Était-ce le cas jusqu'à présent ?

Écrire

13 Pensez-vous, comme Annette (l. 791), que l'insulte est une agression ? Vous répondrez à cette question en développant au moins deux arguments et deux exemples.

14 Le salon des Houllié se transforme en tribunal. Alain et Véronique se font les avocats de leur propre fils. Alain pense qu'il s'agit d'une erreur excusable par la jeunesse de Ferdinand, Véronique pense que la jeunesse n'excuse pas la violence. Développez ces deux tirades d'environ huit lignes chacune, en n'omettant pas de préciser, dans les didascalies, la position du décor, ainsi que les gestes et le ton des personnages.

Chercher

15 Trouvez deux synonymes appartenant aux niveaux de langue courant et soutenu du terme « balance » (l. 797, p. 42).

16 Cherchez dans un dictionnaire étymologique la racine latine du terme « délibérément ». Donnez deux mots de la même famille, en précisant leur sens.

17 Cherchez dans le dictionnaire les différents sens du mot « civilisation ».

Oral

18 Faites une lecture expressive du procès de Figaro, dans la scène 15 de l'acte III du *Mariage de Figaro* de Beaumarchais.

À SAVOIR

LA PAROLE THÉATRALE : LE CONFLIT COMME MOTEUR

Au théâtre, la parole est prépondérante, qu'elle s'exprime sous forme de monologue (tirade durant laquelle un personnage parle seul), de tirade (longue réplique), de réplique ou de stichomythie (échange rapide de répliques très courtes). Par conséquent, se manifestant à travers des dialogues argumentés, allant jusqu'à la polémique, c'est le conflit qui se pose en moteur de l'action. Il peut porter sur des sentiments ou sur des idées, comme dans la pièce de Yasmina Reza. En effet, s'il s'agit tout d'abord de savoir, à l'intérieur de la sphère familiale, quelle solution apporter à la dispute des garçons, la question philosophique sous-tendant le comportement des personnages se pose rapidement : l'homme agit-il selon la morale, c'est-à-dire selon un code qu'il a appris et qui lui dicte le bien et le mal, ou le naturel prend-il forcément le dessus ? C'est ce à quoi tentent de répondre Alain, Véronique, Annette et Michel, monopolisant tour à tour la parole et la scène pour que le débat progresse.

L'IVRESSE

PAGES 51 À 58

Lire

1 Lignes 1024 à 1057 : que se passe-t-il entre Véronique et Michel ?

2 Dans l'expression « une idée john-waynienne de la virilité » (l. 1059), Alain crée un mot à partir du nom propre *John Wayne*. Comment appelle-t-on les mots nouvellement créés ?

3 Que veut dire Alain lorsqu'il affirme que John Wayne et Ivanhoé sont de la même « lignée » (l. 1064, p. 53) ?

4 Page 53, ligne 1072 : relisez et commentez la réplique de Michel.

5 Pages 51-58 : quels sont les deux camps qui s'opposent dans cette scène ? Est-ce encore les Reille contre les Houllié ?

6 Quel type de comique dénote la didascalie des lignes 1094 à 1095 (p. 54) ?

7 Page 56 : quelle figure de style emploie Annette (l. 1149-1150). Quel effet veut-elle produire ?

8 Quelle opinion Alain a-t-il des femmes en affirmant qu'elles « raisonnent trop » (l. 1148, p. 56) ?

9 Comparez les tirades d'Alain (l. 1126-1136) et de Michel (l. 1183-1192). Quelle conception ont-ils de la vie ?

Écrire

10 Écrivez un paragraphe dans lequel vous expliquerez quelles sont les différences entre le cinéma et le théâtre.

Chercher

11 Cherchez des informations sur John Wayne.

Oral

12 Argumentez : dans un discours, Véronique explique en trois arguments pourquoi elle a écrit ce livre sur le Darfour.

À SAVOIR

LE COMIQUE AU THÉÂTRE

Il existe quatre types de comique au théâtre. Le comique de mots s'appuie sur des plaisanteries ou des répétitions (ex. : le mot « défiguré », l. 270-280). Le comique de gestes s'exprime par exemple par des empoignades (ex. : Véronique et son mari, l. 1310). Le comique de caractère repose sur un personnage, comme Michel, ridiculisé par sa phobie des rongeurs. Le comique de situation provient de l'intrigue qui occasionne des quiproquos ou des retournements de situation, comme lorsque la mère de Michel avoue prendre de l'Antril, alors qu'Alain se trouve dans le salon de son fils.

JOHN WAYNE DÉSARMÉ

PAGES 59 À 66

Lire

1 Alain choisit précisément les mots de sa déclaration de presse (p. 59-61). En quoi les mots sont-ils source de polémique dans la pièce ?

2 Quelle est l'importance du langage dans les professions de Véronique et d'Alain ?

3 Page 61 : quelles conceptions de la vie s'opposent (l. 1268-1276) ?

4 Lignes 1309 à 1311 : pourquoi la didascalie indique-t-elle la capitulation de Véronique ?

5 Alain dit que « la morale nous prescrit de dominer nos pulsions » (l. 1334, p. 64). En quoi reprend-il le débat de fond de la pièce ?

6 Alain parle de « la souveraineté des actionnaires » (l. 1373, p. 66). Que signifie cette expression ? La monarchie fait du roi le descendant de Dieu. Qui est le dieu d'Alain ? Quels en sont les descendants ?

Écrire

7 Un collaborateur d'Alain entre dans le salon des Houllié pour demander des précisions à Alain sur le problème de l'Antril. Imaginez la réaction d'Alain et des autres personnages. Écrivez la scène.

Chercher

8 D'où vient l'expression « être citoyen du monde » (l. 1353, p. 65) ?

Débattre

9 Menez un débat en classe sur l'impact du portable sur la vie quotidienne. Un groupe défendra ses aspects positifs, un autre ses aspects négatifs.

À SAVOIR

PERSONNAGES ET CARACTÈRES

Au XVIIe siècle, le personnage de théâtre est un caractère : il correspond à un ensemble de traits physiques, psychologiques et sociaux précis (ex. : dans *L'Avare*, Molière met en scène Harpagon, un vieux bourgeois que l'avarice rend grotesque). Les siècles suivants, le personnage se complexifie et gagne en réalisme. De nos jours, les personnages ont souvent un nom et un prénom, une famille, des préoccupations qui ressemblent à celles du public et, par-dessus tout, ils ont des failles permettant d'autant plus facilement aux spectateurs de s'identifier à eux (ex. : Véronique défend la morale et la culture, mais cède à ses pulsions en bondissant sur son mari).

Lire

1 Alain se réclame de John Wayne (p. 52) : il boit du rhum et hésite à fumer le cigare. À quel objet du cow-boy son portable, dans lequel tient « sa vie entière » (l. 1392, p. 67), fait-il référence ? Quelle opinion Annette a-t-elle sur l'évolution des accessoires masculins ? Relisez sa tirade de la ligne 1422 à 1435 (p. 68).

2 Quel est l'accessoire de prédilection de Michel ? Pour répondre, appuyez-vous sur la réplique de Véronique (l. 1406-1407). Pourquoi est-ce comique, voire grotesque ?

3 Michel aide Alain (p. 66-68) comme il a aidé Véronique (*cf.* étape 5, p. 87). Comment appelle-t-on, dans le récit ou au théâtre, les personnages qui viennent en aide au héros ?

4 Annette rit de la réplique de Véronique (l. 1406-1407), tout comme le spectateur. Quel phénomène propre au théâtre note-t-on ici avec évidence ?

5 Relisez la tirade d'Annette (l. 1422-1438). Quelle conception a-t-elle de l'homme idéal ? Comparez sa tirade avec les réflexions d'Alain sur les femmes pages 56 et 76.

6 Lignes 1462-1463 : que montre la réplique d'Annette ?

7 La fin de la pièce présente l'anéantissement de Véronique et d'Alain (p. 70), jusque-là en position de force. Expliquez les raisons de ce renversement de situation. Qu'en est-il d'Annette ? Quels rôles jouent l'eau et l'alcool dans cette scène ?

8 Lignes 1490 à 1501 : que montrent les répliques d'Annette et d'Alain à propos de la profession de ce dernier ? A-t-il des compétences sur le sujet qu'il défend ?

9 Quel est le dénouement de l'intrigue ? A-t-on trouvé la solution pour résoudre le problème des deux garçons (p. 72-73 et 76) ?

10 Comment Véronique et Michel s'y prennent-ils pour faire le procès d'Annette (p. 74-75) ?

11 En quoi est-il remarquable que ce soit la fille des Houllié qui téléphone à ses parents (l. 1647-1658, p. 77-78) ? Pourquoi Véronique lui raconte-t-elle un mensonge ?

12 En quoi la dernière question posée par Michel correspond bien à l'image du personnage ? Sur quel ton conclut-elle la pièce ?

Écrire

13 Rédigez une critique, c'est-à-dire un article de presse, ayant pour sujet *Le Dieu du carnage*. Présentez tout d'abord la pièce et son auteur (utilisez la présentation de début d'ouvrage). Évoquez ensuite l'intrigue plus en détails, sans en dévoiler le dénouement, de façon à donner aux lecteurs l'envie d'aller voir la pièce. Livrez enfin votre point de vue argumenté sur l'œuvre, dévoilant ce qui constitue selon vous ses points forts et ses points faibles.

14 La fille de Véronique et Michel rentre plus tôt que prévu et trouve ses parents en compagnie des Reille. Ils évoquent ensemble l'altercation des garçons et la disparition du hamster. Écrivez la scène.

Chercher

15 Qu'est-ce que le Ku Klux Klan ?

16 Dans un dictionnaire des symboles, cherchez la symbolique de la tulipe.

Oral

17 Nous avons tous nos héros : John Wayne et Ivanhoé constituent le modèle des hommes, et il semble que Jane Fonda soit celui de Véronique. Quels acteurs ou quels personnages de fiction sont les vôtres ? Faites un sondage dans la classe. Tentez de définir, avec vos camarades, les valeurs véhiculées par les personnages élus.

18 Avec l'aide d'un camarade qui dirigera la mise en espace, jouez la tirade d'Annette, de la ligne 1422 à 1438.

19 Faites le portrait social et psychologique de Michel. Énumérez ensuite les caractéristiques et les qualités du comédien qui prendra en charge le rôle : quelle doit être son apparence physique ? Ses vêtements ? Ses attitudes ? Justifiez vos points de vue.

À SAVOIR

LA STRUCTURE D'UNE PIÈCE DE THÉÂTRE

Une pièce de théâtre commence par l'exposition, qui donne au spectateur les informations dont il a besoin pour comprendre l'action qui va se dérouler, et piquer son intérêt (*cf.* p. 82-83). Vient ensuite le nœud de la pièce, autrement dit le moment où les personnages sont confrontés à différents obstacles qui nouent le conflit jusqu'à le porter à son paroxysme, son acmé. Sa résolution a lieu au moment du dénouement, en demi-teinte dans la pièce de Yasmina Reza, car il n'est ni heureux (les personnages ne parviennent pas à s'entendre), ni réellement malheureux (aucun événement dramatique ne met fin au conflit, et les personnages ne se séparent pas avant la dernière réplique).

LE DIEU DU CARNAGE OU LA DÉMULTIPLICATION DES CONFLITS

« Sans conflits, il n'y aurait pas de théâtre. »
(Ionesco, *Notes et Contre-notes*, 1962)

Dans *Le Dieu du Carnage*, Yasmina Reza met en abîme les conflits. Il y a tout d'abord le conflit opposant les enfants, qui sert d'intrigue à la pièce, entremêlé au choc de la rencontre de deux univers familiaux situés aux confins d'une même bourgeoisie. On lit également l'affrontement de deux philosophies, incarnées par deux caractères : Alain, qui croit au dieu du carnage, autrement dit à la loi du plus fort et à l'impossibilité pour l'homme d'être perfectible, et Véronique, qui au contraire a foi en le progrès qu'offre la culture et qui conduit l'humanité vers un avenir meilleur. En outre, les deux couples ne parviennent pas complètement à faire bloc l'un contre l'autre : le conflit entre époux, matérialisé par les scènes de ménage qui émaillent le huis clos, tiraille les personnages ; et pour cause : chaque couple est composé de deux forces antagonistes, l'homme et la femme. À travers cette démultiplication d'oppositions et un humour parfois grinçant mais toujours présent, se dessine la véritable nature de l'homme, déchiré entre son animalité et sa conscience de créature évoluée, ou, pourrait-on dire en reprenant la fable de La Fontaine, entre la sauvagerie du loup et la bonne éducation de l'agneau. « *Castigat ridendo mores* » : la comédie châtie les mœurs en riant, selon la formule de Jean Santeuil. Le théâtre, plus que tout autre genre littéraire, se nourrit des petites et des grandes misères de la condition humaine, d'ordinaire enfouies en nous-mêmes, qu'il extériorise dans le dialogue avec nos semblables, le transformant en un jeu régi par les rapports de force.

Jean de La Fontaine (1621-1695)

« Le Loup et l'Agneau », *Fables*, livre I, 1668.

À l'époque classique, la liberté de ton est d'autant plus restreinte que les puissants sont invincibles et leur parodie de justice implacable. La Fontaine, sous couvert d'une fable, fait du loup l'arme rêvée du dieu du carnage. Il incarne le pouvoir absolu et l'essence de l'injustice. Il est coupable, mais il n'en a cure. À chacun son rôle naturel : l'agneau est innocent et sympathique, le loup est coupable et détesté.

> **La raison du plus fort est toujours la meilleure :**
> **Nous l'allons montrer tout à l'heure.**
> **Un Agneau se désaltérait**
> **Dans le courant d'une onde pure.**
> **Un Loup survient à jeun qui cherchait aventure,**
> **Et que la faim en ces lieux attirait.**
> **« Qui te rend si hardi de troubler mon breuvage ?**

Dit cet animal plein de rage :
Tu seras châtié de ta témérité.
– Sire, répond l'Agneau, que Votre Majesté
Ne se mette pas en colère ;
Mais plutôt qu'elle considère
Que je me vas désaltérant
Dans le courant,
Plus de vingt pas au-dessous d'Elle,
Et que par conséquent, en aucune façon,
Je ne puis troubler sa boisson.
– Tu la troubles, reprit cette bête cruelle,
Et je sais que de moi tu médis l'an passé.
– Comment l'aurais-je fait si je n'étais pas né ?
Reprit l'Agneau, je tette encor ma mère.
– Si ce n'est toi, c'est donc ton frère.
– Je n'en ai point. – C'est donc quelqu'un des tiens :
Car vous ne m'épargnez guère,
Vous, vos bergers, et vos chiens.
On me l'a dit : il faut que je me venge. »
Là-dessus, au fond des forêts
Le Loup l'emporte, et puis le mange,
Sans autre forme de procès.

Alfred Jarry (1873-1907)

Ubu roi ou les Polonais, joué pour la première fois en 1888 et édité en 1896 dans *Le Livre d'art* (revue de Paul Fort).

Le Père et la Mère Ubu sont deux personnages grotesques qui ont fait date dans l'histoire du théâtre. Le Père Ubu, stupide et méchant roi de Pologne, est un tyran n'utilisant que la force brute pour obtenir ce qu'il désire. C'est un personnage réduit à ses pulsions animales. La Mère Ubu, quant à elle, est l'incarnation de la manipulation psychologique et affective. Les époux sont donc les deux faces d'un même masque profondément immoral et délirant, ignorant de toute culture. Leur couple même serait ubuesque, c'est-à-dire totalement absurde, s'ils n'étaient pas à ce point complémentaires. Dans cet extrait proche du dénouement de la pièce, la Mère Ubu se rend, la nuit, dans la caverne où le Père Ubu s'est réfugié. Elle se fait passer pour une apparition, et cherche une satisfaction toute égoïste, faisant brosser son propre portrait à son mari afin de le manipuler une nouvelle fois.

PÈRE UBU. Ah ! ma gidouille ! Je me tais, je ne dis plus mot. Continuez, madame l'Apparition !

MÈRE UBU. Nous disions, monsieur Ubu, que vous étiez un gros bonhomme !

PÈRE UBU. Très gros, en effet, ceci est juste.

MÈRE UBU. Taisez-vous, de par Dieu !

PÈRE UBU. Oh ! les anges ne jurent pas !

MÈRE UBU *à part.* Merde ! *continuant.* Vous êtes marié, monsieur Ubu.

PÈRE UBU. Parfaitement, à la dernière des chipies !

MÈRE UBU. Vous voulez dire que c'est une femme charmante.

PÈRE UBU. Une horreur. Elle a des griffes partout, on ne sait par où la prendre.

MÈRE UBU. Il faut la prendre par la douceur, sire Ubu, et si vous la prenez ainsi vous verrez qu'elle est au moins l'égale de la Vénus de Capoue.

PÈRE UBU. Qui dites-vous qui a des poux ?

MÈRE UBU. Vous n'écoutez pas, monsieur Ubu ; prêtez-nous une oreille plus attentive. À part. Mais hâtons-nous, le jour va se lever. Monsieur Ubu, votre femme est adorable et délicieuse, elle n'a pas un seul défaut.

PÈRE UBU. Vous vous trompez, il n'y a pas un défaut qu'elle ne possède.

MÈRE UBU. Silence donc ! Votre femme ne vous fait pas d'infidélités !

PÈRE UBU. Je voudrais bien voir qui pourrait être amoureux d'elle. C'est une harpie !

Jean Anouilh (1910-1987)

Les Poissons rouges, © Éditions de la Table Ronde, 1970.

Le drame bourgeois prend des allures burlesques dans la pièce de Jean Anouilh. Une petite fille de quelques mois pleure et renvoie ses parents aux mammifères qu'ils sont. Le langage inarticulé du « tas de chiffons » suffit en effet à fissurer leur assurance d'adulte, faisant ressortir à coup de poncifs (selon lesquels les filles préfèrent leur père, seule la mère est certaine d'être génitrice, ou l'homme doit avoir la place de mâle dominant au sein de la famille), le « naturel », autrement dit, l'animal, qui sommeille en eux.

CHARLOTTE *essaie de la calmer un instant en vain et la lui repasse.* Non. Décidément, elle veut être avec toi. Reprends-la !

Dès que le tas de chiffons est dans les bras d'Antoine, les cris s'arrêtent. Il constate, satisfait.

ANTOINE. J'ai tout de même une certaine influence masculine sur elle.

CHARLOTTE, *qui regarde, amère, vexée.* C'est comme toutes les filles. Elle préfère son père. Ce que j'ai fait pour elle, ma vie risquée, mes seins flétris par les tétées, rien ne compte ! Elle préfère son père. Hé bien, soit ! Garde-la. Moi, je dors. *Elle se recouche.*

ANTOINE. Ah non ! Ce serait trop facile ! Reprends-la et donne-lui le sein. Cela lui changera les idées. C'est ta fille, après tout !

Il a remis d'autorité le tas de chiffons dans les bras de Charlotte.

CHARLOTTE, *berçant le bébé qui s'est remis à crier, furieuse.* Ce n'est pas la tienne, peut-être ?

ANTOINE. Je l'espère. Quoique ce soit une chose dont on n'est jamais sûr.

CHARLOTTE, *sortant furieusement son sein.* Monstre ! Mufle ! Goujat ! Tu l'aurais mérité ! C'est trop tard pour celle-là, mais tu l'aurais mérité ! Bois, mon ange ! C'est le lait de maman. Papa n'en a pas.

Le bébé crie et refuse le sein.

CHARLOTTE. Tu l'as montée contre moi ! Elle refuse le sein de sa mère, l'ingrate !

ANTOINE, *retapant le lit et se couchant.* Quoi qu'il en soit, moi, je suis un traditionnaliste. Je suis pour la mère au foyer. C'est elle qui élève les enfants. Moi, je défends l'entrée de la caverne, avec ma grosse massue ; je vais à la chasse et je reviens le soir avec un quartier d'auroch saignant sur l'épaule pour nourrir tout le monde. Je dors. [...]

Le tas de chiffons hurle de plus en plus ; elle [Charlotte] hurle aussi, le secouant abominablement.

CHARLOTTE. Tu vas te taire ? Tu vas te taire ? Tiens, vas le retrouver, ton père puisque tu l'aimes plus que moi ! Tu verras comment il te fera téter, lui !

Elle a remis de force le bébé dans les bras d'Antoine, surpris.

ANTOINE, *le bébé dans les bras.* Elle crie avec moi aussi, maintenant !... Tu lui as donné de déplorables habitudes ! Son éducation est fichue !

Le dieu du carnage ou la démultiplication des conflits

Edward Albee (né en 1928)

Qui a peur de Virginia Woolf ?, représenté pour la première fois au Billy Rose Theater à Broadway le 13 octobre 1962, *L'Avant-Scène*, Éditions Robert Laffont, 1975, adaptation de Jean Cau.

« Ce qu'il y a d'ennuyeux dans l'amour, c'est que c'est un crime où l'on ne peut pas se passer d'un complice. » Cette réflexion de Baudelaire dans *Mon cœur mis à nu* s'applique au théâtre d'Edward Albee. Le couple et la famille sont une microsociété dans laquelle les conflits s'épanouissent comme dans une partie de cartes tragique et comique à la fois, dans laquelle chacun, tour à tour, désavoue son partenaire, bluffe, tente de désarçonner l'autre partie et y cherche un allié. Dans cette pièce, George, professeur d'histoire, est marié à Martha, la fille du directeur de l'université. Ils invitent, alors que la nuit est déjà bien entamée, Nick, nouveau professeur de biologie, et Honey, son épouse.

NICK, ***montrant une peinture abstraite.*** **Qui… qui a peint ce… ?**

MARTHA. Ça ? Oh ! c'est de…

GEORGE. Une espèce de Grec moustachu sur lequel Martha s'est jetée, une nuit…

HONEY, ***pour essayer de faire diversion.*** **Ho, ho, ho !… Ho ! Ho !…**

NICK, ***regardant le tableau.*** **Je trouve qu'il y a… On y sent…**

GEORGE. Une force tranquille ?

NICK. Non…, plutôt…

GEORGE. Ah !… ***(Un temps.)*** **Un calme vibrant… Peut-être ?**

NICK, ***comprenant que George se paie sa tête, mais restant poli et calme.*** **Non, je voulais plutôt dire…**

GEORGE. C'est ça : disons une force vibrante de tranquillité ?

HONEY. Chéri, on se moque de toi…

NICK, *froid.* Je le sais.

Bref silence.

GEORGE, *sincère.* Je suis désolé… *(Nick hoche la tête avec condescendance.)* En vérité, ce tableau représente l'intérieur de la tête de Martha.

MARTHA. Ha, ha, ha !… Offre un verre à ces enfants, George. Qu'est-ce que vous voulez boire, mes petits ? Hein ?

NICK. Honey ? Qu'est-ce que tu veux ?

HONEY. Je ne sais pas, chéri… Un peu de cognac, peut-être. *(Elle a son petit rire.)*

GEORGE. Du cognac ? Sec ? Très bien, très bien. Et vous ?….

NICK. Eh bien… Un whisky… si ça ne vous dérange pas.

GEORGE, *en versant les boissons.* Déranger ? Non, non, ça ne me dérange pas. Ca ne me dérange absolument pas… Martha ? Et pour toi, qu'est-ce que ce sera ? Alcool à brûler ?

MARTHA. Ouais.

GEORGE, *ton de conversation mondaine et aimable.* Les goûts de Martha, en ce qui concerne les boissons, se sont beaucoup simplifiés. Avec les années…, ils se sont… épurés… […]

MARTHA. Eh ! il arrive, mon alcool à brûler ?

GEORGE, *se dirigeant à nouveau vers le bar.* […] Avec les années, Martha a appris à ne pas mélanger n'importe quoi… Maintenant, elle sait qu'on met le lait dans le café, le citron sur le poisson… et que l'alcool pur *(il tend le verre à Martha)*, tiens, mon ange, est réservé à la très pure Martha. *(Il lève son verre.)* À votre santé.

INTERVIEW EXCLUSIVE

Pour la collection « Classiques & Contemporains », Yasmina Reza a accepté de répondre aux questions de Sylvie Coly, professeur de lettres et auteur du présent appareil pédagogique.

Sylvie Coly : Yasmina Reza, vous êtes à la fois comédienne, metteur en scène, auteur et réalisatrice. Vous avez vous-même mis en scène *Le Dieu du carnage* en janvier 2008 à Paris, après que la pièce a été montée par Jürgen Gosch à la Schauspielhaus de Zurich en 2006, et reprise par le Berliner Ensemble. Pourquoi avoir tenu à monter vous-même cette pièce, et pourquoi avoir attendu deux ans ?

Yasmina Reza : Je vous remercie de tous les titres que vous me donnez mais si vous le permettez, je me définirais avant tout comme un écrivain. Je conçois les activités autres comme des formes dérivées d'écriture.

Jürgen Gosch avait « commandé » cette pièce. Non pas le sujet, ni rien de précis, mais il voulait créer une pièce de moi au Schauspielhaus. (Il avait déjà mis en scène deux pièces précédentes.) Je l'ai écrite dans cette perspective et, chemin faisant, en cours de travail, l'idée m'est venue que je la mettrai moi-même en scène en France. J'avais depuis un certain temps l'envie de monter une de mes pièces mais l'évidence s'est produite avec celle-ci.

Le temps que ça a pris n'est qu'une question de concordance entre mon emploi du temps, la disponibilité des acteurs et du théâtre.

S. C. : *Le Dieu du carnage* est la deuxième pièce publiée dans la collection « Classiques & Contemporains », après *« Art »*, qui remporte toujours un franc succès auprès des élèves. Quel regard portez-vous sur le fait d'être étudiée en classe ?
Y. R. : J'en suis profondément heureuse. C'est un grand privilège de pouvoir toucher, par le biais de l'étude et de la langue, une génération nouvelle.

S. C. : Pensez-vous, comme Véronique, qu'il « existe un art de vivre ensemble », et quelle définition donnez-vous ici au mot « art » ?
Y. R. : Question que les traducteurs ont dû se poser ! Véronique emploie le mot « art » là où, personnellement, je ne l'utiliserais pas. Un personnage se révèle essentiellement par ses choix sémantiques.

S. C. : La pièce est un huis clos. Certains détails du décor, comme par exemple les livres d'art de Véronique ou le portable d'Alain, ont une importance capitale dans l'économie dramatique. Selon vous, tous les détails scéniques doivent-ils être aussi précisément et rigoureusement choisis que les mots du texte ?
Y. R. : Tous les auteurs ont une façon très personnelle d'écrire les didascalies. Certains sont très précis, d'autres moins. Pour ma part, je serais plutôt minimaliste. Je me contente de préciser les éléments indispensables et incontournables pour l'action dramatique ; le portable et les tulipes « jouent ».

S. C. : *Le Dieu du carnage* fait l'objet d'un film réalisé par Roman Polanski. Est-ce pour éviter de vous sentir dépossédée de votre œuvre, comme Marguerite Duras à la suite du tournage de *L'Amant* par Jean-Jacques Annaud, que vous avez tenu à participer à l'écriture du scénario ?
Y. R. : Non, pas du tout. Roman Polanski souhaitait que nous adaptions ensemble le texte.

S. C. : Quel nouveau regard apporte l'adaptation cinématographique sur la pièce initiale ?
Y. R. : Le scénario est très proche de la pièce. Le film est en cours de tournage. Pour le moment, je n'ai vu que des prises de vues et des rushes. Ils sont excitants et revèlent déjà une grande tension, mais je ne peux pas juger de l'ensemble.

BIBLIOGRAPHIE ET FILMOGRAPHIE

• D'autres œuvres de Yasmina Reza

Théâtre :

– *Conversation après un enterrement*, Acte-Sud Papiers, 1992.
– *La Traversée de l'hiver*, Acte-Sud Papiers, 1992.
– *« Art »*, Albin Michel, 1994, paru dans la collection « Classiques & Contemporains » n° 40, Magnard, 2001.
– *L'Homme du hasard*, Acte-Sud Papiers, 1999.
– *Trois Versions de la vie*, Albin Michel, 2000.
– *Une pièce espagnole*, Albin Michel, 2004.

Récit :

– *Hammerklavier*, Albin Michel, 1997.

• Héroïsme et regards sur l'autre

Romans :

– Walter Scott, *Ivanhoé*, 1819.
– William Golding, *Sa Majesté des mouches*, 1954.
– Michel Tournier, *Vendredi ou la Vie sauvage*, 1971.
– Driss Chraibi, *La Civilisation ma mère*, 1972.

Cinéma :

– Yves Robert, *La Guerre des boutons*, 1912.
– Delmer Daves, *La Flèche brisée*, 1949.
– John Ford, *Rio Grande*, 1950, avec John Wayne dans le rôle du lieutenant-colonel York.

INTERNET

– Écouter la critique de Fabienne Pascaud, qui concerne la mise en scène de Yasmina Reza de sa propre pièce, en février 2008 pour *Télérama* :
http ://www.telerama.fr/scenes/25247-le_dieu_du_carnage_une_piece_de_yasmina_reza_commentee_par_fabienne_pascaud.php ?xtor=RSS-18
– Lire la critique du *Dieu du carnage* de Laurence Liban, pour *L'Express*, du 4 février 2008 :
http ://www.lexpress.fr/culture/scene/theatre/le-dieu-du-carnage_473541.html

VISITE

Le théâtre de votre ville, ou le théâtre Antoine, 14 boulevard de Strasbourg, 75010 Paris, où fut monté *Le Dieu du carnage* en 2008 (http://www.theatre-antoine.com/).

SÉRIE « LES GRANDS CONTEMPORAINS PRÉSENTENT »

D. Daeninckx présente *21 récits policiers*
L. Gaudé présente *13 extraits de tragédies*
A. Nothomb présente *20 récits de soi*
K. Pancol présente *21 textes sur le sentiment amoureux*
É.-E. Schmitt présente *13 récits d'enfance et d'adolescence*
B. Werber présente *20 récits d'anticipation et de science-fiction*

Adam, *Je vais bien, ne t'en fais pas*
Alain-Fournier, *Le Grand Meaulnes*
Anouilh, *L'Hurluberlu – Pièce grinçante*
Anouilh, *Pièces roses*
Anouilh, *La Répétition ou l'Amour puni*
Balzac, *La Bourse*
Barbara, *L'Assassinat du Pont-Rouge*
Begag, *Salam Ouessant*
Bégaudeau, *Le Problème*
Ben Jelloun, Chedid, Desplechin, Ernaux, *Récits d'enfance*
Benoit, *L'Atlantide*
Boccace, Poe, James, Boyle, etc., *Nouvelles du fléau*
Boisset, *Le Grimoire d'Arkandias*
Boisset, *Nicostratos*
Braun (avec S. Guinoiseau), *Personne ne m'aurait cru, alors je me suis tu*
Brontë, *L'Hôtel Stancliffe*
Calvino, *Le Vicomte pourfendu*
Castan, *Belle des eaux*
Chaine, *Mémoires d'un rat*
Colette, *Claudine à l'école*
Conan Doyle, *Le Monde perdu*
Conan Doyle, *Trois Aventures de Sherlock Holmes*
Corneille, *Le Menteur*
Corneille, *Médée*
Cossery, *Les Hommes oubliés de Dieu*
Coulon, *Le roi n'a pas sommeil*
Courteline, *La Cruche*
Daeninckx, *Cannibale*
Daeninckx, *Histoire et faux-semblants*
Daeninckx, *L'Espoir en contrebande*
Dahl, Bradbury, Borges, Brown, *Nouvelles à chute 2*
Defoe, *Robinson Crusoé*
Diderot, *Supplément au Voyage de Bougainville*
Dorgelès, *Les Croix de bois*
Dostoïevski, *Carnets du sous-sol*
Du Maurier, *Les Oiseaux et deux autres nouvelles*
Du Maurier, *Rebecca*
Dumas, *La Dame pâle*
Dumas, *Le Bagnard de l'Opéra*
Feydeau, *Dormez, je le veux !*
Fioretto, *Et si c'était niais ? – Pastiches contemporains*

Gaudé, *La Mort du roi Tsongor*
Gaudé, *Médée Kali*
Gaudé, *Salina*
Gaudé, *Voyages en terres inconnues – Deux récits sidérants*
Gavalda, Buzzati, Cortázar, Bourgeyx, Kassak, Mérigeau, *Nouvelles à chute*
Germain, *Magnus*
Giraudoux, *La guerre de Troie n'aura pas lieu*
Giraudoux, *Ondine*
Gripari, *Contes de la rue Broca et de la Folie-Méricourt*
Gripari, Dubillard, Grumberg, Tardieu, *Courtes pièces à lire et à jouer*
Grumberg, *Les Vitalabri*
Havel, *Audience*
Higgins Clark, *La Nuit du renard*
Higgins Clark, *Le Billet gagnant et deux autres nouvelles*
Highsmith, Poe, Maupassant, Daudet, *Nouvelles animalières*
Hoffmann, *L'Homme au sable*
Hoffmann, *Mademoiselle de Scudéry*
Huch, *Le Dernier Été*
Hugo, *Claude Gueux*
Hugo, *Théâtre en liberté*
Ionesco, *Rhinocéros et deux autres nouvelles*
Irving, *Faut-il sauver Piggy Sneed ?*
Jacq, *La Fiancée du Nil*
Jarry, *Ubu roi*
Johnson, *La Colline des potences*
Kafka, *La Métamorphose*
Kamanda, *Les Contes du Griot*
King, *Cette impression qui n'a de nom qu'en français et trois autres nouvelles*
King, *La Cadillac de Dolan*
Kipling, *Histoires comme ça*
Kipling, *Le Livre de la jungle*
Klotz, *Killer Kid*
Leblanc, *Arsène Lupin, gentleman-cambrioleur*
Leroux, *Le Mystère de la chambre jaune*
Lewis, *Pourquoi j'ai mangé mon père*
London, *Construire un feu*
London, *L'Appel de la forêt*
Lowery, *La Cicatrice*
Maran, *Batouala*
Marivaux, *La Colonie* suivi de *L'Île des esclaves*
Mérimée, *Tamango*
Michalik, *Le Cercle des illusionnistes*
Michalik, *Edmond*
Michalik, *Le Porteur d'histoire*
Molière, *Dom Juan*
Molière, *George Dandin*
Molière, *Le Sicilien ou l'Amour peintre*
Murakami, *L'éléphant s'évapore* suivi du *Nain qui danse*
Musset, *Lorenzaccio*
Némirovsky, *Jézabel*
Nothomb, *Acide sulfurique*
Nothomb, *Barbe bleue*
Nothomb, *Les Combustibles*

Nothomb, *Métaphysique des tubes*
Nothomb, *Péplum*
Nothomb, *Le Sabotage amoureux*
Nothomb, *Stupeur et Tremblements*
Pergaud, *La Guerre des boutons*
Perrault, Mme d'Aulnoy, etc., *Contes merveilleux*
Petan, *Le Procès du loup*
Poe, Gautier, Maupassant, Gogol, *Nouvelles fantastiques*
Pons, *Délicieuses frayeurs*
Pouchkine, *La Dame de pique*
Reboux et Muller, *À la manière de...*
Renard, *Huit jours à la campagne*
Renard, *Poil de Carotte* (comédie en un acte), suivi de *La Bigote* (comédie en deux actes)
Reza, *« Art »*
Reza, *Le Dieu du carnage*
Reza, *Trois versions de la vie*
Ribes, *Trois pièces facétieuses*
Riel, *La Vierge froide et autres racontars*
Rouquette, *Médée*
Sand, *Marianne*
Schmitt, *Crime parfait et Les Mauvaises Lectures – Deux nouvelles à chute*
Schmitt, *L'Enfant de Noé*
Schmitt, *Hôtel des deux mondes*
Schmitt, *Le Joueur d'échecs*
Schmitt, *Milarepa*
Schmitt, *Monsieur Ibrahim et les fleurs du Coran*
Schmitt, *La Nuit de Valognes*
Schmitt, *Oscar et la dame rose*
Schmitt, *Ulysse from Bagdad*
Schmitt, *Vingt-quatre heures de la vie d'une femme*
Schmitt, *Le Visiteur*
Sévigné, Diderot, Voltaire, Sand, *Lettres choisies*
Signol, *La Grande Île*
Stendhal, *Vanina Vanini*
Stevenson, *Le Cas étrange du Dr Jekyll et de M. Hyde*
Twain, *Les Aventures de Tom Sawyer*
Uhlman, *La Lettre de Conrad*
Vargas, *Debout les morts*
Vargas, *L'Homme à l'envers*
Vargas, *L'Homme aux cercles bleus*
Vargas, *Pars vite et reviens tard*
Vargas, *Sous les vents de Neptune*
Vercel, *Capitaine Conan*
Vercors, *Le Silence de la mer*
Vercors, *Zoo ou l'assassin philanthrope*
Voltaire, *L'Ingénu*
Wells, *La Machine à explorer le temps*
Werth, *33 Jours*
Wilde, *Le Crime de Lord Arthur Savile*
Zola, *Thérèse Raquin*
Zweig, *Le Joueur d'échecs*
Zweig, *Lettre d'une inconnue*
Zweig, *Vingt-quatre heures de la vie d'une femme*

Recueils et anonymes

90 poèmes classiques et contemporains

Les Aventures extraordinaires d'Adèle Blanc-Sec

Ceci n'est pas un conte et autres contes excentriques du XVIII*e siècle*

Ces objets qui nous envahissent : objets cultes, culte des objets

Cette part de rêve que chacun porte en soi

La condition féminine – Littérature d'idées

Contes populaires de Palestine

La Dernière Lettre – Paroles de Résistants fusillés en France (1941–1944)

Histoires vraies – Le Fait divers dans la presse du XVI*e au* XXI*e siècle*

La Farce de Maître Pierre Pathelin

Les Grands Textes du Moyen Âge et du XVI*e siècle*

Les Grands Textes fondateurs

Informer, s'informer, déformer ?

Initiation à la poésie du Moyen Âge à nos jours

Je me souviens

Nouvelles francophones

Poèmes engagés

Pourquoi aller vers l'inconnu ? – 16 récits d'aventures

La Presse dans tous ses états – Lire les journaux du XVII*e au* XXI*e siècle*

La Résistance en poésie – Des poèmes pour résister

La Résistance en prose – Des mots pour résister

Sorcières, génies et autres monstres – 8 contes merveilleux

SÉRIE BANDE DESSINÉE (en coédition avec Casterman)

Beuriot et Richelle, *Amours fragiles – Le Dernier Printemps*

Bilal et Christin, *Les Phalanges de l'Ordre noir*

Comès, *Silence*

Ferrandez et Benacquista, *L'Outremangeur*

Franquin, *Idées noires*

Manchette et Tardi, *Griffu*

Martin, *Alix – L'Enfant grec*

Pagnol et Ferrandez, *L'Eau des collines – Jean de Florette*

Pratt, *Corto Maltese – La Jeunesse de Corto*

Pratt, *Saint-Exupéry – Le Dernier Vol*

Stevenson, Pratt et Milani, *L'Île au trésor*

Tardi et Daeninckx, *Le Der des ders*

Tardi, *Adèle Blanc-sec – Adèle et la Bête*

Tardi, *Adèle Blanc-sec – Le Démon de la Tour Eiffel*

Tardi, *Adieu Brindavoine* suivi de *La Fleur au fusil*

Tito, *Soledad – La Mémoire blessée*

Tito, *Tendre banlieue – Appel au calme*

Utsumi et Taniguchi, *L'Orme du Caucase*

Wagner et Seiter, *Mysteries – Seule contre la loi*

Couverture
Conception graphique : Marie-Astrid Bailly-Maître
Photographie : Pascal Victor/ArcomArt

Intérieur
Conception graphique : Marie-Astrid Bailly-Maître
Édition : Charlotte Cordonnier
Réalisation : Nord Compo, Villeneuve-d'Ascq

www.magnard.fr
www.classiquesetcontemporains.com

Achevé d'imprimer en février 2021 par Rotolito en Italie
N° éditeur : MAGSI20210007 - Dépôt légal : Avril 2011